Henry Moore

David Sylvester

FREDERICK A. PRAEGER, Publishers
New York · Washington

Books That Matter
Published in the United States of America in 1968
by Frederick A. Praeger, Inc., Publishers
111 Fourth Avenue, New York, N.Y. 10003
Copyright in London, England, by David Sylvester, 1968
All rights reserved

Library of Congress Catalog Card Number: 68-8254

Designed by Gilvrie Misstear
Printed in Great Britain

To Adrian Stokes

Preface

The present volume is the revised edition of a monograph originally published by the Arts Council of Great Britain in association with the retrospective exhibition at the Tate Gallery, selected by the author, on the occasion of Henry Moore's seventieth birthday.

Nearly all the photographs of sculptures are by the artist, and I am greatly indebted to him for having taken a number expressly for this publication. Also for his patient answers to numerous questions about his methods and intentions.

The choice and arrangement of the illustrations were made in collaboration with Joanna Drew of the Arts Council, the editor; Gilvrie Misstear, the designer; and Anne Seymour, my assistant.

Anne Seymour also provided substantial help in the overall planning of the book, collaborated in compiling the chronology, and contributed numerous insights and improvements to the main body of the text. Bernard Meadows painstakingly communicated information on the basis of which I have revised some datings accepted in previous publications, some of them my own, and have added or amended details about Moore's methods and career. Charles Mitchell and Andrew Forge contributed valuable suggestions. I am indebted to my students at Swarthmore College for certain interpretations of Moore's imagery.

I am grateful to Gabriel White, Director of Art of the Arts Council, for his encouragement; to Anthony Bell and John Taylor of Lund Humphries for their advice; to Mrs Betty Tinsley, the artist's secretary, for help in gathering photographs. As to my editor, there is no rhetoric in saying that without her the book could not have existed.

London, September 1968   A. D. B. S.

Contents

Chronology

1898 30 July. Born at Castleford, Yorkshire, a small mining town near Leeds. He was the seventh child of Raymond Spencer Moore (1849–1921) and Mary Baker (1860–1944). His father, who was of Irish stock, came from Lincolnshire, his mother from Staffordshire. For two or three generations the men on both sides of the family had worked on the land or in the mines. Raymond Spencer Moore began work at the age of 9 on a farm, but for most of his life was a coal-miner. Self-educated, he was an active socialist and trade unionist.

1910 Won a scholarship from his elementary school to Castleford Grammar School. Here he was to meet with great help and encouragement from the art mistress, Alice Gostick. The enthusiasm of his headmaster, T. R. Dawes, for English church architecture introduced him to the Gothic carvings in neighbouring churches at Methley and Adel.

1915 Became a student teacher, despite his ambition to be a sculptor, in accordance with his father's wish that he should first qualify in a secure profession.

1916 Took up a teaching post in September at his old elementary school.

1917 Joined up in February as a private in the 15th London Regiment (Civil Service Rifles). Sent to France in early summer. Gassed in the battle of Cambrai. Sent back to hospital in England early in December.

1918 In March became a P.T. and bayonet instructor with the rank of lance-corporal. Redrafted to France in November.

1919 Demobilized in February and resumed his old teaching post a month later. In September secured an ex-servicemen's education grant and entered Leeds School of Art, where he studied for two years.

While at Leeds read Roger Fry's *Vision and Design* and visited Sir Michael Sadler's collection.

1921 Won a Royal Exhibition Scholarship in Sculpture: in September entered the Royal College of Art.

Residence in London enabled him to make constant visits to the British Museum. He was particularly drawn to Egyptian, Sumerian, Etruscan, Mexican and African Sculpture.

1922 Began to spend his vacations at Stiffkey in Norfolk, where he started doing sculpture out of doors.

About this time read the Vorticist magazine *Blast* and Ezra Pound's biography of Henri Gaudier-Brzeska.

Away from the College made his first direct carvings, in stone and in wood—influenced by primitive and archaic sculpture and by Gaudier and Epstein.

1923 At Whitsun made the first of more or less annual visits to Paris. Saw the Cézannes in the Pellerin collection. Took his diploma at the Royal College and spent the next year doing advanced studies.

Carvings, mainly in stone, of heads and figures.

1924 Awarded Royal College of Art Travelling Scholarship, but, on completing his third year as a student at the College, was appointed instructor in the Sculpture School for a term of seven years, to teach two days a week, and postponed going abroad in order to take temporary charge of the department.

Carvings included first reclining figure.

1925 In France and Italy from the end of January till mid-July, visiting Paris, Rome, Florence, Pisa, Siena, Assisi, Padua, Ravenna and Venice, returning via Paris. Impressed by the Indian sculpture in the Guimet Museum, by Giotto and Masaccio, by early Renaissance portrait busts, late Michelangelo and, ambivalently, Donatello.

1926 Exhibited for the first time, in a mixed show at the St George's Gallery.

First sculptures in concrete. Neo-classical reclining female figures, perhaps influenced by Maillol. First influence of Cubism.

1927 Helped to form a small group of young artists for an exhibition at the Beaux-Arts Gallery.

Continued with neo-classical figures and other carvings influenced by primitive and cubist art. Made a duck in cast concrete reflecting Brancusi's influence.

1928 First one-man exhibition: the Warren Gallery.

Began work on first public commission – a relief carving for a façade of the new Underground Station building, St James's Park.

1929 In July married Irina Radetzky, a painting student at the Royal College of Art. Moved into a studio at 11a Parkhill Road, Hampstead.

Continued to work mostly on stone carvings of reclining figures, half-lengths, mother and child groups, masks and heads. First reclining figure influenced by the Chacmool from Chichén Itzá. Mexican influence also in heads and half-lengths. First cubist-inspired use of a cavity in a figure. At about this time started to collect pebbles.

1

1930 Elected to the 7 and 5 Society (1920–35). Members in the 1930s included Nicholson, Hepworth, Hitchens, Piper. Published his first article: a statement in a series on contemporary English sculptors, *Architectural Association Journal*, May. First article published on his work: by R. H. Wilenski, *Apollo*, December.

Mostly stone carvings: same subjects. Continued Mexican influence, but some softening of forms.

1931 First of his one-man shows at the Leicester Galleries. Catalogue preface by Jacob Epstein, whom he had known since 1926–7. First article on him published abroad: by Gustav Delbanco, *die Weltkunst*, April. Bought a cottage at Barfreston, Kent, for work during college vacations.

Mostly stone carvings with emphasis on mother and child groups and half-lengths. First biomorphic abstract compositions and reliefs.

1932 Despite violent criticism in the press of his show at the Leicester Galleries and calls for resignation from the staff and Old Students Association of the Royal College, Sir William Rothenstein, the Principal, had urged Moore not to give up his post there. However, on expiry of his contract this year, rather than apply for renewal, he accepted the offer, at a lower salary, of starting up a sculpture department and teaching two days a week at Chelsea School of Art, under H. S. Williamson.

Stone and wood carvings, both figurative and biomorphic-abstract. Further softening of forms. Growing tendency for space to cut through the block.

1933 Member of Unit 1, founded this year by Paul Nash. Other members included Hepworth, Armstrong, Burra, Nicholson, Wadsworth and the architects Wells Coates and Colin Lucas.

Biomorphic forms, with increasing incorporation of space.

1934 Left Barfreston to take a cottage with a large field (where he could work out of doors) at Kingston, near Canterbury. First monograph published on him: *Henry Moore, Sculptor*, by Herbert Read.

Continued with biomorphic abstract carvings: now more geometrical with some sharp edges and flat planes, so that curved forms appear cut through in section. First multiple-piece compositions.

1935 About this time started making sketch-models for sculptures. Began working with an assistant, Arthur Jackson. His subsequent assistants have included Bernard Meadows (1936–9 and intermittently 1947–53), Reg. Butler, Anthony Caro, Phillip King, Isaac Witkin.

Abstract carvings in stone and wood.

1936 A founder member of the Surrealist group in England; though not profoundly committed to its doctrines (the following year he declared: 'The violent quarrel between the abstractionists and the surrealists seems to me quite unnecessary'), he felt closer to Surrealism than to the alternative allegiance, Constructivism. Made a tour of cave paintings in the Pyrenees and at Altamira; visited Madrid, Toledo, Barcelona. Exhibited in the International Surrealist Exhibition at the New Burlington Galleries.

Stone sculpture now very square – solid, monolithic, abstract forms with shallow surface carving and incised linear designs. Two elm wood carvings of reclining figures, with opened-out forms.

1937 Softened square forms in stone. First stringed figures in wood.

1938 Carved his first opened-out reclining figure in stone. Stringed figures in wood and terracotta.

1939 Stopped teaching for the duration of the war, as the Chelsea School was evacuated from London.

Carved a third, larger, elm reclining figure, further opened-out. Made a number of small sculptures in lead, modelled in wax and cast at the Kingston studio: several reclining figures, several stringed figures, and his first sculpture with internal and external forms.

1940 Returned to London studio. Later moved into 7 Mall Studios, which Barbara Hepworth and Ben Nicholson had evacuated on their move to Cornwall. When the studio was damaged by bombing in October, took the house at Perry Green, Much Hadham, Hertfordshire, where he has lived since.

Concentrated mainly on drawing. In the spring stopped making sculpture completely owing to difficulty of obtaining materials in wartime. First shelter drawings, September. Subsequently appointed official war artist (until 1942).

1941 First retrospective exhibition: Temple Newsam, Leeds. Appointed a Trustee of the Tate Gallery. Has since served continually on numerous boards, including the National Gallery, the Arts Council, the Royal Fine Art Commission, the National Theatre.

Worked on shelter drawings.

1942 Went to Castleford for a fortnight in January, under the auspices of the War Artists' Advisory Committee, to observe miners at the coal face, then made a series of drawings. Resumed drawings for sculpture, including studies of draped figures.

1943 First one-man exhibition abroad: Buchholz Gallery, New York (drawings).

Commissioned to carve a Madonna and Child for St. Matthew's, Northampton. Made numerous sketch-models and started on the carving.

1944 Sketch-models for stone and bronze family groups with draped figures, originating in a commission for Impington Village College (Cambridge). This was never carried out owing to lack of funds, but two of the designs were later executed life-size.

1945 Created Honorary Doctor of Literature at the University of Leeds – first academic award. He has since received Honorary Doctorates from numerous British and foreign universities, including Harvard, Oxford and Cambridge.

Worked in a wide range of styles, often using ideas from wartime drawings. Sketch-models for family groups, abstract and naturalistic reclining figures and a group of three standing figures. Autumn: started a draped reclining figure in stone, a memorial to Christopher Martin, first Art Administrator at Dartington Hall. Simultaneously began another large elm reclining figure.

1946 Birth of his daughter, Mary. Retrospective exhibition at the Museum of Modern Art, New York – first of over 100 retrospective shows abroad. Visited New York for the first time.
Worked mainly on reclining figures.

1947 Gave up teaching.
Started carving the over-life-size group of three draped standing figures in stone.

1948 Served on the committee of the first London County Council Open Air Exhibition of Sculpture, held at Battersea Park. Won the International Sculpture Prize at the 24th Venice Biennale: first of several international awards. First visit to Italy since 1925: made a number of visits thereafter.
Started bronze family group commissioned by the Barclay School, Stevenage: first life-size bronze. Began carving a Madonna and Child commissioned for St Peter's, Claydon, Suffolk.

1949 Bronze seated draped figures, some with very flat forms.

1950 Mainly bronze, a few lead, sculptures. Small rocking-chair mother and child groups. Over-life-size standing figure, made up of slender, abstract bone forms. Helmet-heads and openwork heads. Worked on commission from the Arts Council for a large bronze reclining figure for the 1951 Festival of Britain.

1951 First trip to Greece: visited Athens, Mycenae, Olympia, Corinth and Delphi. First retrospective in London: Tate Gallery.
Abstract sculptures with internal/external forms.

1952 Began work on commission for a stone screen and a bronze reclining figure for the new Time-Life Building, London. First use of clinging classical drapery. Numerous bronzes with pointed or flattened forms or parts broken away or left unfinished. Started the King and Queen.

1953 Was ill for most of the summer, and was operated on for removal of a kidney stone. First visit to Mexico; also to Brazil.
Started large wood version of upright internal/external sculpture, also large bronze internal/external reclining figure.

1954 Completed large bronze figure of a warrior and worked on stone carving of a family group for Harlow. Began work on commission to design a relief in brick for the Bouwcentrum, Rotterdam. From about this time virtually gave up making drawings for sculpture and came increasingly to use stones and bones in composing sketch-models.

1955 Companion of Honour.
Began a series of free-standing totemic sculptures with interlocking biomorphic forms related to the Bouwcentrum designs.

1956 In response to the commission to make a sculpture for the forecourt of the new UNESCO headquarters in Paris, worked on several trial compositions for figures in a setting to be carried out in bronze. Finally decided to make a marble reclining figure.

1957 Visited Italy to begin carving the UNESCO figure at the stoneyard at Querceta, near Carrara; it was completed on the site. Worked on somewhat naturalistic bronzes of nude and draped seated and reclining women, and of a falling warrior.

1958 First abstract forms in a setting. Large bronzes of draped women.

1959 Small bronze figures of animals and birds. Large upright bronze reliefs of standing torsos with interlocking bone forms. First two-piece bronze reclining figure. Began another large elm reclining figure, after a sketch-model of 1954 (completed 1964).

1960 Worked on second, larger, two-piece bronze reclining figure; landscape metaphor increasingly pronounced. Began large abstract bronze reclining mother and child with internal/external forms.

1961 First exhibition at Marlborough Fine Art.
Continued with rock-like two-piece reclining figures; began a large three-piece figure. First large knife-edge sculptures.

1962 Began work on Locking Piece. Polished bronze abstract sculptures: streamlined forms with sharp edges.

1963 Order of Merit.
Began work on commission for large two-piece reclining figure for Lincoln Center, New York. Made a second large three-piece figure, with smooth, architectonic, forms. While on holiday at Forte dei Marmi in Italy, near the Carrara quarries, began a carving in marble, later finished in England.

1964 Mostly worked on Lincoln Center commission and the larger version of the Locking Piece. Further polished bronze sculptures.

1965 Bought a cottage at Forte dei Marmi, as a summer studio for stone carving.
Abstract carvings in marble. Completed a large abstract to be cast in polished bronze for a square in Toronto and for the forecourt of a new museum by Mies in Berlin. Small works in polished bronze. Started work on a commission for a sundial for The Times building, London and a large abstract for Chicago University.

1966 Abstract multiple-piece compositions carved in marble. Abstract sculptures in polished bronze.

1967 Marble carvings including a mother and child. Started a large marble carving with internal and external forms. Completed a large bronze abstract environmental sculpture.

1968 Abstract multiple-piece compositions with interlocking bone and stone forms.

3

The Reclining Figure

Two-thirds of Moore's sculptures of full-length figures are reclining figures. With one exception they are women. Most of them are nudes, but though they lie with knees apart or thighs apart, their overall pose doesn't betoken the availability commonly implied in reclining female nudes. Their bearing, especially the set of head on shoulders, is more male than female. Sometimes their posture recalls the Mexican rain-god, Chacmool; it frequently recalls the river-gods.

Personifications such as river-gods of nature's flowing energy are traditional pretexts for sculptures of reclining figures. Moore's figures, of course, represent nothing but themselves, but are made to look as if they themselves had been shaped by nature's energy. They seem to be weathered, eroded, tunnelled-into by the action of wind and water. The first time Moore published his thoughts about art, he said that the sculpture which moved him most gave out 'something of the energy and power of great mountains'.[1] Later, on the subject of making holes in figures: 'the mystery of the hole – the mysterious fascination of caves in hillsides and cliffs'.[2] He evidently perceives the energy and power and mystery he seeks less in specifically human properties than in properties also attributed to forms of landscape.

Even his drawings from life can reveal as much (56) when he draws a seated model from a viewpoint on a level with her knees, sometimes almost her ankles, defining her legs with strong black marks of the pen while adumbrating her chest and head with a paler and paler wash, so that she looms up like a mountain whose summit is almost lost in the distance of the sky. There are also carvings of upright figures (17, 23) which have a certain mountainous quality. But broadly speaking it is obvious that, especially in sculpture, a figure which is to be the equivalent of landscape is apt to have a horizontal pose.

But the primary ideal is 'energy and power': Moore's reclining figures are not supine; they prop themselves up, are potentially active. Hence the affinity with river-gods: the idea is not simply that of a body subjected to the flow of nature's forces but of one in which those forces are harnessed.

The shelter drawings do include supine figures, in fact sleeping figures. There is also one sculpture, unlike any other, which almost lies back flat – the slab-like carving in Corsehill stone of 1934–5 (5). It recalls a flat slab covering a tomb. It also evokes death through the compactness of its form: the limbs seem bound to the body as in mummies. Or, rather, as in a Lazarus. For one side of the slab is raised off the ground, and the head is strangely upright: it is as if the figure were urging itself back into life. A drawing of 1936 (55) places a similar figure on a block, like an effigy on a sarcophagus. The grave is evoked again by some of the figures reclining in the shelters (99, 100): their settings are like sepulchres, their drapes like cerements, and sometimes a trick of style in the way they are drawn suggests the skeleton beneath the skin. The shelterers seen waking from a sleep take on an air of rising blearily from death.

Aside from its metaphoric possibilities, the reclining figure is the ideal vehicle for Moore's most constant formal preoccupations. Moore thinks from the ground up. When he was teaching in art schools he used to encourage his students to start a life-drawing of a standing figure with the feet and work upwards. It was essential that the figure should be firmly grounded. For him, gravity comes first, and however much he may erode the mass, weight is his point of departure. A figure close to the ground gives him that.

A reclining figure, furthermore, 'is free and stable at the same time'.[3] Moore's ideal is to 'turn an inert block into a composition which has a full form-existence, with masses of varied size and section conceived in their air-surrounded entirety, stressing and straining, thrusting and opposing each other in spatial relationship – being static, in the sense

1 Reclining woman 1930, length 37 in.

that the centre of gravity lies within the base (and does not seem to be falling over or moving off its base) – and yet having an alert dynamic tension between its parts'.[4] It is practically inconceivable that this ideal could be realized in a sculpture of a single figure that was not a reclining figure. Possibly this is one reason why so many of Moore's vertical figurative sculptures are not of one figure but two: mother and child.

And then there is Moore's avowed and manifest insistence on asymmetry – something not easily reconciled with an insistence on static poses. Though a reclining figure can be posed to present a symmetrical image when seen end-on – and Moore very occasionally uses such a posture (6) – there is no such difficulty in posing it, as there is with a seated, a standing, a kneeling, a crouching, figure, so that it is asymmetrical from every angle. In ensuring that it is, Moore creates an opposition between the two halves of the body which tends to undermine their continuity. Sometimes the pose is anatomically untenable because the head end and the leg end are behaving incompatibly.[5] It is hardly surprising that Moore has been led to sever the connexion between the parts, arriving at figures composed of separate masses – first in 1934 (4), and since 1959 repeatedly (11, 12).

Certainly, Moore's preoccupation with asymmetry harmonizes with his present obsession with Michelangelo and veneration for the pedimental figures from the Parthenon. But in 1935 he listed 'the great sculpture of the world' as the Sumerian, Early Greek, Etruscan, Ancient Mexican, Fourth and Twelfth Dynasty Egyptian, Romanesque, and early Gothic.[6] Most of these have a distinct bias towards symmetry, none more so than the Mexican, which was 'unsurpassed in my opinion by any other period of stone sculpture'.[7] He admired its 'approach to a full three-dimensional conception of form'[8] and the 'full three-dimensional existence' of Sumerian sculpture.[9] And yet he had lately declared that 'Sculpture fully in the round has no two points of view alike. The desire for form completely realized is connected with asymmetry.'[10] Admittedly it is not quite clear from this what Moore understood by asymmetry. If he intended it in a strict geometric sense, then the sculpture he prized most highly was not symmetrical, but in that case he was enunciating a truism: any piece of pottery, let alone figurative art, that is aesthetically alive is not absolutely symmetrical, any more than a human face is. What matters is that most of his 'great sculpture of the world' is, as sculpture goes, symmetrical, that is, by comparison with, say, Mannerist or Baroque or Hellenistic or classical Greek sculpture: these are the kinds of sculpture that truly have 'no two points of view alike'. And it is evident that Moore did feel that the sculpture he most admired was excessively symmetrical from his point of view. 'As to the "four-square" posture of most primitive figures, I think that this is a limitation on the artist.'[11] He may not have said this in print till 1951, by which time his earlier preferences had been modified by a growing appreciation of classical and Renaissance art, but in his work the thought was manifest by 1930.

In 1929 and 1930 he carved two reclining figures – probably his outstanding early works – which were inspired by the Toltec-Mayan Chacmool from Chichén Itzá (144).

The 1930 figure (1), despite the change of sex, is almost a paraphrase of it. But with these differences: the Chacmool head is turned at right angles to the body, the Moore head looks back over one shoulder; the Chacmool head is symmetrical, the Moore head asymmetrical; the torso in the Chacmool has the same direction as the legs and is supported by both elbows, with the forearms placed symmetrically across the body, the torso of the Moore is twisted out of line and its weight is supported by one elbow; the legs in the Moore are spread wider.

The figure carved in 1929 (2) is even closer to the Chacmool in the massive, blocked-out character of its shapes. But here too the symmetry and frontality are rejected, except for the unusual turn of the head at right-angles to the axis of the block. This is no insignificant feature to have copied: the consequential uprightness of the head and neck gives both figures the peculiarly alert look they have. On the other hand, Moore has as it were taken the parallel legs of the Chacmool and turned them onto their sides, transferring the body's weight from the buttocks to one hip, has accordingly twisted the torso to one side and put one arm on the ground as a support, and has also brought the free arm up to support the head. Whereas the Mexican figure's body and limbs form a compact unit with a single direction, Moore, while preserving all its chunkiness, has reconciled this with contrapposto. His figure's pose, indeed, rather resembles that of Michelangelo's Dawn (145). If the resemblance was not at all intended, it still may not have been at all fortuitous.

Moore at this time had been very much

torn between the allegiance to primitive art formed through visits to the British Museum during his years, 1921–4, at the Royal College and the involvement in the European tradition which he had come to feel, despite himself, during a six months' stay in Italy (reluctantly embarked-on) as a travelling scholar in 1925. 'For about six months after my return I was never more miserable in my life. Six months' exposure to the master works of European art which I saw on my trip had stirred up a violent conflict with my previous ideals. I couldn't seem to shake off the new impressions, or make use of them without denying all I had devoutly believed in before. I found myself helpless and unable to work. Then gradually I began to find my way out of my quandary in the direction of my earlier interests. I came back to ancient Mexican art in the British Museum. I came across an illustration of the *Chacmool* discovered at Chichén Itzá in a German publication[12] – and its curious reclining posture attracted me – not lying on its side but on its back with its head twisted around. Still, the effects of that trip never really faded. But until my shelter drawings during the war I never seemed to feel free to use what I learned on that trip to Italy in my art – to mix the Mediterranean approach comfortably with my interest in the more elementary concept of archaic and primitive peoples. I feel the conflict still exists in me. And I ask myself, is this conflict what makes things happen or will a synthesis eventually derive?'[13] Moore was talking around 1946, since which time he has certainly felt 'free to use' what he 'learned on that trip to Italy', sometimes to the exclusion of his other interests. But he may when he talked

have been underestimating his earlier capacity 'to mix the Mediterranean approach comfortably' with the influence of primitive art.

The facts suggest that the very theme of the reclining figure was a legacy of his Italian journey. There were few reclining figures in the round among the sculpture he looked at most in his student days – Egyptian, Sumerian, African, Mexican, and other primitive and archaic art—apart from the Etruscan. Among his twenty-five recorded sculptures made before going to Italy there is one reclining figure (of a man). In Italy he would have seen any number of reclining figures, Renaissance and antique. During the two years after his return he made four sculptures of reclining women, quite academically classical in manner. Then came his great discovery of the *Chacmool* – a discovery reflected in his work for years after. Yet his first response to it was neither to accept its aesthetic nor to combine this with expressly contemporary elements – that came later (6) – but to combine it with elements of the Mediterranean tradition. The surprising resemblance to the *Dawn* of the first carving based on the *Chacmool* is there in the general disposition of the forms, especially the looming upper leg, and in details such as the shape of the breasts and their relation to the shoulders – and where Moore has slightly modified the pose by placing the left hand at the back of the head instead of on the shoulder, his alternative is Michelangelesque. Three years later he made a figure in carved reinforced concrete (3), which again resembles the *Dawn* in its pose and this time is curiously Michelangelesque in style.[14]

But by now Moore was beginning to take a

direction suggested by Picasso, and his subsequent reclining figures have been variations on the human form rather than representations – except when, since 1945, he has produced a compensatory classicizing piece (96). Yet the more abstract sculptures too have poses which are the prerogative of the Mediterranean tradition. In some cases the prototypes are again Michelangelesque, as in a figure (12) the position of whose legs and the tilt of whose head recalls the *Night* (148), and another (13) with a remarkable resemblance to the stricken St Paul in the Pauline Chapel fresco of the *Conversion* (147). Others seem to reflect antique prototypes directly. There are figures lying sideways, their chests facing outwards, their slightly parted legs almost parallel and looking from some angles as if cut off at the knees (9), which recall the Parthenon figure of a river-god known as the *Ilissus* (146). There are figures leaning back, supported on one elbow, legs apart with knees slightly bent (7), which recall the Parthenon figure known as the *Dionysus* (143). There are figures lying sideways with torsoes very upright and one knee more bent than the other (8, 71) which recall the Roman river-gods in the Piazza del Campidoglio (142).[15] Notwithstanding his long-held belief that 'the realistic ideal of physical beauty in art which sprang from fifth-century Greece was only a digression from the main world tradition in sculpture,'[16] Moore's handling of his most constant theme seems to have responded constantly to the classical 'digression.'

2 Reclining figure 1929, length 33 in.

3 Reclining figure 1932, length 43 in.

4 Four-piece composition: reclining figure 1934, length 20 in.

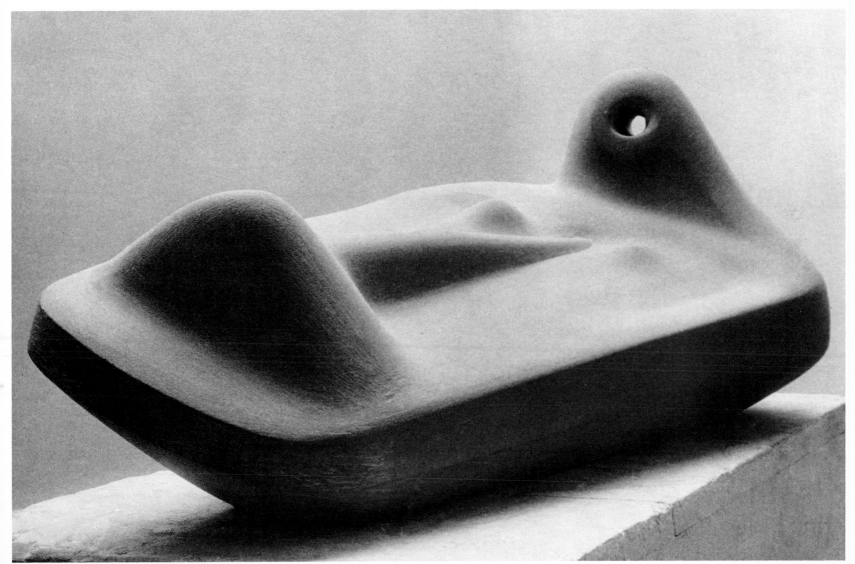

5 Reclining figure ?1934–5, length 24½ in.

6 Reclining figure 1937, length 33 in.

7 Reclining figure 1939, length 81 in.

13

8 Recumbent figure 1938, length 55 in.

9 Reclining figure 1959–64, length 90 in.

15

10 Reclining figure 1951, length, 90 in.

11 Two-piece reclining figure No. 1 1959, length 76 in.

12 Two-piece reclining figure: sketch-model No.4 1961, length 8¼ in.

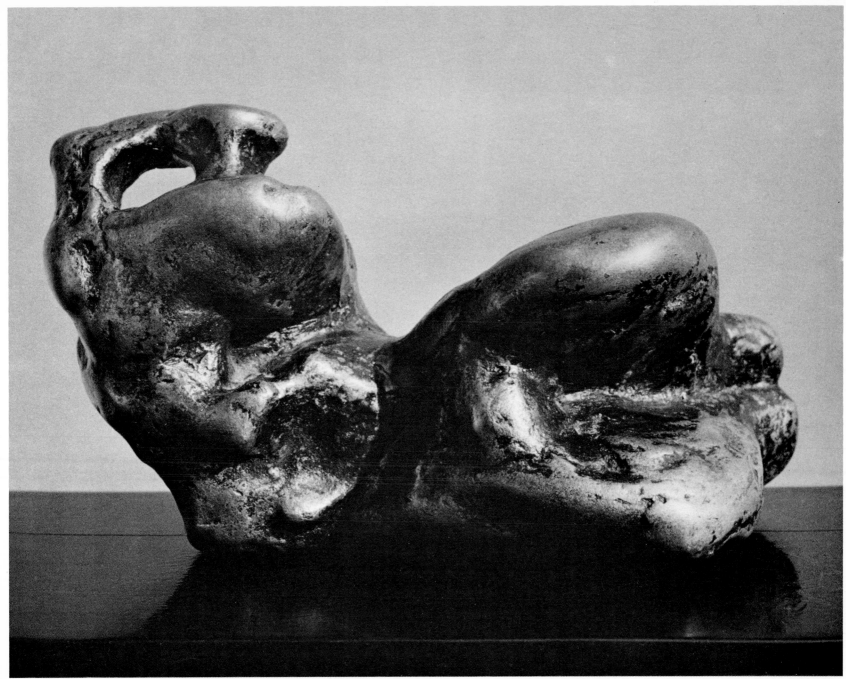

13 Reclining figure: Bunched 1961, length 5¾ in.

The Mother and Child

Moore's other major figurative theme was already conspicuous in his earliest work. The three carvings of a mother and child, each relating the figures in a different way (16, 17), which he made before going to Italy[1] are certainly his most ambitious works of the time and probably the most convincing (none more so than the first of them, in which the child seems to be struggling out of a narrow gap between the crouching mother's legs and arms as if in some strange parable or myth of birth – an image that does not derive from the work's Egyptian and Pre-Columbian sources). Yet in the next five years, during which he completed fifty sculptures, the theme appears in just three miniature carvings (four to six inches high) and a larger piece of a *Suckling Child* (27). Whereas Italy opened his eyes to the reclining figure, it may be he was paralysed by the sight of all those Madonnas, perhaps because they were not simply Art. Then, in the next three years, 1930–2, he did thirteen carvings of a *Mother and Child* (18, 19, 20, 21, 22) and another *Suckling Child* – one in four of his sculptures of the period.

Here again, as with the reclining figure, he was able to gain impetus once he could see how to impose a style derived from the Mexican, the Sumerian and the like onto a subject more dominant in Europe than elsewhere.

Here again, as with the reclining figure, he found a theme which suited his desire for asymmetry and a complex interaction of contrasting masses.

The mother-and-child series of 1930–2 was concurrent with his first experiments in a more abstract idiom, and from 1933 till 1940 (when the war stopped him from making sculptures for three years) all the sculpture that he did was somewhat abstract, more precisely, post-Picassoid. One way Moore found to translate the theme into more abstract terms was to create a single mass fusing schematic images of a larger and a smaller figure – this in two stone carvings and in three modelled stringed sculptures (14). Another way was to allude to the theme through a relationship between two wholly separate abstract forms, as in the stone *Bird and Egg* – a mother and child at a different evolutionary level – and the Pynkado wood *Two Forms* (26), which is clearly an elemental image of the mother-and-child relationship, among other things.

In 1940–1 the shelter drawings brought back figurative images of mother and child, but with the figures draped (98, 100). These led on in 1943 to the series of sketch-models for a carving of a *Madonna and Child* commissioned for St Matthew's, Northampton and executed in 1943–4 (23): later one of the

variant models (102) was used for a carving done in 1948–9 for St Peter's, Claydon. The commission presented Moore with new formal as well as iconographic problems (not to mention those raised by suddenly working under ecclesiastical patronage): the sketch-models were his first sculptures of clothed figures; they also entailed realizing the mother as a full-length figure – a task he had tended to avoid. Apart from the early block-statue – the compactness of which by-passed the problem – Moore had previously made only one full-length woman with a child, a seated woman (22): the others had been half-lengths, or occasionally three-quarter-lengths, of what generally appear to be standing figures. But he was now helped to deal with this problem by having to deal with the other, for the drapery enabled him to treat the seated woman's legs as a single mass. It may well be that her posture in the Northampton version reflects Moore's long-standing admiration for the headless archaic Greek draped seated figures in the British Museum (152). If these weathered statues are compared with the Moore at a stage in its execution where its forms were equally blurred (153), there is a marked resemblance in their bearing. This may be stretching a point. But Moore did write of trying to invest his piece with 'a sense of complete easiness and repose'[2] two years after describing the archaic figures as 'seated in easy, still naturalness, grand and full like Handel's music'.[3] As to medieval or Renaissance prototypes, the Claydon version looks back to early-fourteenth-century Gothic, perhaps French more than Italian, but the Northampton version's antecedents are harder to pin down. To relate it to very early Jacopo della Quercia would be excessively cute. Perhaps it owes something to Italian painting. Moore's first hero among painters is Masaccio; in the 30s he had cited 'a Masaccio madonna' – along with Michelangelo's drawings' – as a paradigm of 'monumental grandeur'[4]; and there are significant resemblances in design – the position of the child in the Virgin's lap, the way she holds one of His hands – between the Northampton *Madonna* and the Masaccio *Virgin and Child Enthroned* in the National Gallery (150). At the same time, there are equally relevant links with Giotto (149), and with Raphael (151).

In 1944–5 Moore made a series of fourteen sketch-models of a *Family Group* – a seated man and woman with one or two children (24) – and one of a group of two women with a child (103). In 1946 his daughter was born: he made several life drawings of the baby, a few of the mother and child. Since then he has realized some of the *Family Group* models on a larger scale – two of them life-size – but has shown no profound interest in the mother-and-child theme in its traditional form. In the 1950s he produced a number of lighthearted, mostly small, pieces of mothers – some of them in rocking chairs – playing with their infants, which only go to show how he is not a Matisse or a Miró, is

portentous or nothing. He also made a strange, angular expressionistic sculpture with the child as a rapacious dog threatening the breast of a mother trying to hold it at arm's length. Oblique, half-hidden images of aggressive eating are recurrent and powerful in Moore's work, but brought into the open the image seems gratuitous. Where he has done major work on the theme over the last twenty years has been in images wherein the child is not a separate human entity, is still a part of the mother.

In 1953–4 he carved a large upright composition in elm wood, *Internal and External Forms*, in which an elemental human form is contained like an embryo within a slightly anthropomorphic sort of shell which seems to be actively protecting it as well as housing it. A reclining counterpart on a smaller scale, with the head emerging from the shell, gives a reptilian sort of image which leaves little room for connotations of mother and child; when Moore came to enlarge this, he ultimately eliminated the internal form, leaving the shell empty (73). But the image was developed in the *Reclining Mother and Child* of 1960–1 (25), possibly the greatest of Moore's works in bronze. The combination of reclining figure with mother and child had previously appeared in a few drawings of the late 1920s, but there it was simply a mother holding an infant. On the other hand, there is a sheet of ideas for metal sculpture drawn in 1939 (34) in which one image (the central figure in the fifth row down) does seem to have anticipated the 1960–1 bronze. Here the form of the child is not yet human – is an entity at once more primitive and more potent – and is retained within the reclining woman's

hollow body. A very recent carving of a *Mother and Child* (15, 28) focuses on the child's relation to the breast, as did those early sculptures of a suckling child, but very differently. These early works physically isolate the breast with the child attached to it; the late work presents a half-length figure of the mother, but the whole sculpture is a metaphor of the child's attachment to the breast. The early works partake of the idea of a close-up, inasmuch as they take a part of the mother's body out of its context; the late work has all the visual properties of a close-up. It is a key characteristic of many of Moore's carvings of the 60s that, unlike his previous carvings, they seem to imply close-up vision, as if the observer were almost enveloped in the object rather than perceiving it out there, at a distance: compare, for example, the large elm *Reclining Figure* of 1959–64 (9) with that of 1939 (7); or, say, a stone-carving of *Two Forms* of 1966–7 (42) with one of 1934 (47). And the late *Mother and Child* possesses – what the *Suckling Child* sculptures do not – the ambiguity of close-up vision as to what one is looking at. From the front (28), the child's head might also be a breast and the oval shape which stands for the mother's face might be a mouth approaching it – and in fact is the same shape as stands for the child's head in the *Reclining Mother and Child* (80). From the back (15), the tumescent breast thrusting out to touch the shoulder of the child might also be a child's head burrowing into a breast. An alternative form presents itself of the child's incorporation in the mother – as against enclosure, a merging of identities.

16 Mother and child 1922, height 11 in.

Mother and child 1924–5, height 22½ in.

18 Mother and child 1931, height 14 in.

19 Mother and child ?1930–1, height 16 in.

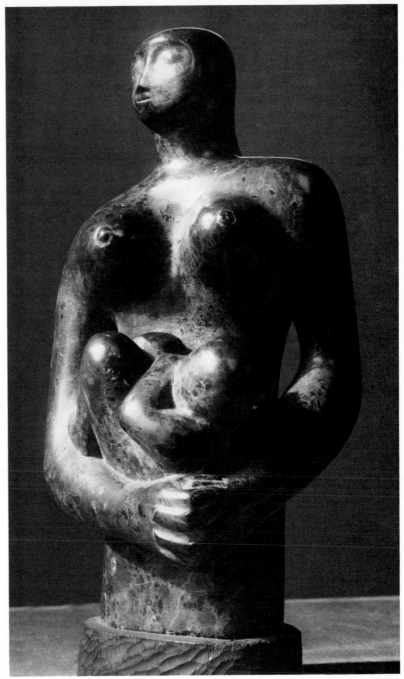

20 Mother and child 1931, height 18 in.

21 Mother and child 1931, height 8 in.

22 Mother and child 1932, height 37 in.

23 Madonna and Child 1943–4, height 59 in.

24 Sketch-model for Harlow family group 1944, height 6⅛ in.

25 Reclining mother and child 1960–1, length 86½ in. (detail)

26 Two forms 1934, length 21 in.

27 Suckling child 1927, length 17 in.

33

28 Mother and child 1967, length 51¼ in.

Correspondences

Early in 1931 Moore carved a *Composition* in blue Hornton stone (31), a tentative piece, which was his first sculpture in a more or less abstract idiom. For two years he produced work of this kind concurrently with figurative work, then almost exclusively work of an abstract kind from 1933 till 1940. Whereas the figurative pieces of the early 30s tend to retain something of that squareness of form inspired by Mexican art – though they do become increasingly curvilinear between 1930 and 1932 – the early abstract pieces (32, 33) have the serpentine forms characteristic of the language of ambiguous biomorphic shapes which was current in the work of such artists as Arp, Picasso, Miró, Tanguy. (Basically this language was a continuation of Art Nouveau, except that there it had mainly suggested plant forms, now, mainly animal forms. Indeed, the plant forms persist in Arp's imagery, even dominate it till about 1920. If there is one key-work in the evolution of the common language, it is probably Brancusi's *The Princess* (156) of 1916.) From 1934 however, Moore's abstract pieces were becoming less sinuous, tending to revert to a squarer kind of form (53, 62).

Going abstract was primarily a consequence of the Brancusi revolution. Brancusi's 'special mission', as Moore saw it, had been to eliminate an overgrowth in European sculpture since the Gothic of 'all sorts of surface excrescences which completely concealed shape'.[1] If shape were to be asserted, it could be more conspicuous if not immediately associated with a reclining woman, a mother and child, a girl with clasped hands – if the sculpture presented itself as a more autonomous entity. Furthermore, this entity could be given a form that would evoke a multiplicity of associations and so imply the notion of metamorphosis – a possibility with which Brancusi was concerned only intermittently, if at all, but which become central for Arp and Miró and Tanguy, for Picasso at moments, and for Moore. But, if Moore's forms were those of a common language, there is no need to look beyond Picasso's work alone for his specific sources. A pair of abstract low reliefs, mixing biomorphic and geometric shapes, which he made in 1931 are curiously reminiscent in composition of certain Picasso *papiers collés* of 1912–14. The initial *Composition* of 1931 looks as if it must have been based on a Picasso sculpture variously known as *Figure* and *Metamorphosis* (155), made in 1928 in plaster and immediately reproduced in *Cahiers d'Art*,[2] which Moore saw regularly. Like the Picasso, the Moore is a full-length standing, though squat, figure with a tiny head which looks like some grotesque animal; its shapes are similar; it makes a similar use of linear signs incised in the surface; it has a similar open space near the top which is similarly surmounted by a form like a handle – though in the Picasso this seems to represent a long neck, in the Moore it is an arm held up to the head. Picasso made no other sculpture quite like this, but he produced a quantity of drawings and paintings in 1927–9 which have similar forms and in many cases are sculptural in conception, so that if it so happened that Moore missed seeing the sculpture reproduced he could still have deduced a sculpture like it from the related paintings and drawings.[3] These undoubtedly influenced further works by Moore in the next two or three years and via these the mainstream of his work thereafter.

Some carvings of 1932–4 (33, 47) resemble Arp more closely than Picasso. This happens when Moore's forms are more compact than usual: his general tendency, like Picasso's and unlike Arp's, is to penetrate volumes with voids. Again, his actual shapes are usually much more like those of Picasso than of Arp – tense and muscular where Arp's are gentle and fleshy. Moreover, the conformation of Moore's images almost always has a specific model in the human body. While he was doing his most abstract sculptures, he was still constantly drawing from life and teach-

29 Two-piece sculpture: Pipe, 1966 length 37 in.

ing drawing and modelling from life, and these activities were not something apart. Even his most ambiguous pieces were usually conceived as full-length figures (4, 5, 6, 31) or half-lengths (32) or heads-and-shoulders (33) or heads (53). Though many of Arp's sculptures are torsos or half-lengths, others of his 'human concretions' are totally free compositions of anatomical allusions (167), while many pieces relate to plants much more than to the body. Moore, like Picasso, is an anthropocentric artist, which Arp, like Brancusi, is expressly not.

Where Moore's art is totally unlike Picasso's is in its absence of wit, of the sharply incongruous image. Moore's metamorphic forms reveal marvellous and unsuspected likenesses between disparate things, but the revelation is like that of some elemental truth: once recognized, it seems inevitable; it may not lose its mystery, but it does lose its surprise; it seems right and natural, reasonable, not outlandish and questionable. Compare two characteristic sets of variations on the human figure, each realized as drawings as if of sculptures assembled from a mixture of organic and man-made parts: Picasso's several pages of standing figures called *An Anatomy*, dating from 1933[4] (157), and Moore's sheet of reclining figures, *Ideas for sculpture in metal*, 1939 (34). In the Picasso series, the parts include chairs, planks, fruit, vegetables, sand-trays, beakers, balls on strings, a pillow, a hoop, a cog-wheel, a flower-pot, a bladder, a bench, a wedge, a sausage, a fruit dish, bread, piping, nails, door handles and a string of sausages. Anything can be anything. Altogether more homogeneous, the Moore variations look like

curious implements, also look as if they might be made of bones. Now, Picasso himself had composed several 'bone-figures' in paintings and drawings of around 1930, but Moore reduces the figure to what might be an assemblage of just three or four bones – perhaps developing a conceit advanced in a lead statuette of a *Reclining Figure* of 1938 (35) wherein the two legs are transformed into a single bone. And the form of these bones is that of bones which can be held in one hand. So the figure becomes an object on that scale – a hand-held articulated structure, perhaps with movable parts: something to be picked up and handled like a tool. Yet, like the human figure, an articulated assemblage of bones. The transformation has a kind of logic.

Free association produces significant results when congruity of structure is discovered in things or situations which are incongruous in their character or context. Art which discovers unexpected correspondences will tend to emphasize either the incongruity which makes them remarkable or the congruity which makes them viable, and with Moore the focus is generally on the structural affinity. If we fail to recognize that the head of Picasso's sculpture of a baboon consists of two toy motor cars, we are not getting the message. With Moore it is not so central to the message what went on in the artist's mind. If told, for example, that the *Three Points* of 1939 (37) had been inspired by a painting, one might hazard a guess that this was one of those Picassos of the *Guernica* period with a woman's or a horse's mouth open in agony and a thrusting tongue with the form of a conical spike

(158): Moore's adaptation would have been to close the jaws so that they impinged more on the tip of the spike. And, considering Moore's relationship to Picasso plus the *réclame* of those particular Picassos at the time the sculpture was made, it is possible that Moore unconsciously derived the spike from Picasso. Furthermore, images of threatening mouths are not uncommon in Moore's work, and no doubt such an image is part of the latent content of this particular work. Nevertheless, the painting which was in fact Moore's source of inspiration was the School of Fontainebleau double-portrait of Gabrielle d'Estrées and her sister in the bathtub (159). The fastidious pinching of Gabrielle's nipple between her sister's pointed forefinger and thumb gave Moore the idea of making a sculpture in which three points would converge so that they were only just not touching.[5] The sheet of studies (made in 1939 though signed 1940) (36) in which the idea for *Three Points* crystallized contains a wide range of variations on the theme of points meeting. Mostly they resemble shells, but four of them are figures which have sharply pointed breasts matched by a second pair of pointed forms, like their reflection, coming up to meet them. In the *Reclining Figure* of the previous year which has a bone in place of legs (35), there are two similar pairs of pointed forms, but the upward-thrusting pair are directed like pincers at one of the breasts, as if this were about to be bitten by the mouth of a fish-like creature incorporated in the figure of the reclining woman. However, when Moore came to adapt the similar image of the plucking fingers in the double-portrait, he reversed the direction of the pincers: instead of their coming from the opposite direction to the point they converge on, all three points stem from the same source. This change brings in a different range of evocations – such as the tongue nipped by the teeth, such as a sting within a sheath, such as a membrane on the point of being pierced – but it seems certain that the conscious motivation for the change was to create a compact and cohesive structure.

In this case Moore began from a specific image which he saw as the paradigm of a type of physical situation. That situation is embodied in the resultant sculpture along with suggestions of other quite different situations; the particular image which started him off has disappeared. *Three Rings*, of which he carved two versions in 1966–7, was another conception, like *Three Points*, unlike anything he had tried before. Only, this time the stimulus was not something seen, but a formal problem to which he set out to discover a solution. He wanted to make, as a present for his daughter, a ring with three openings which could be fitted on a finger in three different ways. His first two attempts failed to come off: as he worked on a third, he noticed how the three rings, rolling up against one another on the bench, tended to fit together. He decided to make a carving of three such rings, and went on to make a medium-sized version in rosa aurora marble (38, 39) and then a very large version in red Soraya marble (74). While he was carving the first, the delicate pale pink colour of the stone gave him the idea that the curves of the outer surfaces should be like the cheeks of a girl's bottom. He was not conscious that he was also making forms whose inner shapes and surfaces suggest her internal anatomy. The red Soraya version is an almost unaltered enlargement yet an altogether different image. The dominating scale, the harsh red-brown colour of the marble, its look of density and hardness, exclude the erotic implications of the earlier version, with its intimate scale, the soft translucent blush of the marble, its pliable, yielding look. Obviously the forms retain their uterine association, but this now serves to suggest something like giant eggs from which large reptiles might have hatched.

The associations which Moore's sculptures evoke recurrently divide into four categories: parts of the human body; parts of animals; landscape; natural objects. Occasionally there is a suggestion of a man-made object: some that have occurred to Moore himself while working on a sculpture are a pipe (29), a bridge (132), a shoe (6), a toy 'bomb'[6] (129), a sparking-plug (37).

Natural objects come frequently to mind, though their range is limited. Very occasionally there is a suggestion of fruits, flowers, fungi, but for the most part the objects evoked are hard: bones, shells, pebbles, flints, boulders, fossils; also, in a number of bronzes of the last ten years, tree trunks and jagged rocks. Such images overlap, of course, with the suggestion of landscape that is almost ever-present in Moore's more complex pieces. The idea that a figure could be a range of mountains was a conscious factor at least as far back as 1930, when Moore wrote of mountains as a sculptural ideal[7] and carved the *Reclining Woman* in green Hornton stone (1).[8] In the second half of the 1930s he was carving his first figures penetrated with holes (7, 8) and writing of 'the mysterious fascination of caves in hillsides and cliffs'.[9] Hillsides was the more appropriate thought for the works of the period; cliffs came into their own in the rough-hewn bronzes of the late 50s and 60s (11, 41). In these later pieces the landscape imagery is more deliberately cultivated than before. It is even based at times on landscape paintings – Monet's Etretat pictures, Seurat's *Bec du Hoc* – as well as, less consciously, on memories of particular places seen in reality: Adel Crag in Yorkshire, which he visited as a boy, is an acknowledged model,[10] as are the slag heaps which were ubiquitous where he grew up; another model might be the Old Harry Rocks offshore near Bournemouth, where he frequently spent summer holidays in the 50s. In some of these later pieces – the *Two-piece Reclining Figure No.2* of 1960, for example – the landscape feeling tends to overwhelm the figure: the tension between human image and landscape image is lost; the sculpture looks like a sculpture of a rock-formation which – as rocks do or clouds do or burning coals do – happens to suggest a figure.

Animals have been explicit subjects for several clearly representational sculptures: dog, horse, goat, snake, bird. Among the abstract sculptures, several are more related to animal than to human forms: the *Bird Basket* (94) is indeed a bird; one of the key images in the *Locking Piece*, for Moore, is an elephant's foot (123); there is a small bronze called *Slow Form: Tortoise* (128). Other sculptures are almost equally suggestive of animal and of human forms: the first of his abstract pieces is a sort of standing figure, but his own nickname for it is 'Elephant in an armchair' (31); the next such piece, the *Composition* of 1931 in Cumberland albaster, is a human half-length resembling some such creature as an octopus; the *Composition* of 1932 in African wonderstone (33) is a human head-and-shoulders and something like a seal. In several sculptures of whole human figures, a part of a woman's body is also a part of an animal: for example, the head of a fish or reptile forms the abdomen of one reclining figure (35), one breast of another (30); in one of the late divided figures (40), the throat is a bird's throat and the middle section evokes the protruding head and forelegs of a giant tortoise.

The parts of the human body which are most often isolated as unidentified forms or appear, magnified, in whole figures or half-figures in places where they are not in reality, are not structural elements: these – it is a matter of that reasonableness which distinguishes Moore from Picasso – tend to stay in their normal relationship to one another. The parts which are subject to being irrationally isolated, magnified, displaced – and this, almost invariably, without conscious knowledge – are the mouth and the genitals. *Three Points* suggests lips and a tongue; in the Pynkado wood *Two Forms* (26) the larger form is a predatory mouth, as well as a grasping hand and a protective shell; in the *Two-piece Reclining Figure No. 1* the legs appear from certain angles (88) to be huge open jaws; in a small *Stringed Figure* of 1939 (93) which is intended as the top half of a reclining figure, the thorax is a gaping mouth with fangs. The female genitals are imaged frequently, in abstractions such as the rosa aurora *Three Rings* and the Pynkado wood *Two Forms* (136), and in the tunnelled forms of reclining figures (30): they are precisely imaged; it is not at all a matter of indiscriminately seeing holes as sexual symbols. Phallic imagery occurs mostly in sculptures of the last ten years. The phallus never appears as an isolated image – unless one indiscriminately sees tall upright shapes (118) as sexual symbols – but only in conjunction with forms that signify the female. It rears up in front of her (11), burrows into her (29), is enclosed within her (80). But there is no more powerful embodiment of sexual confrontation in Moore's work than one presenting no such specific imagery – the *Two Forms* of 1966–7 in red Soraya marble, which are like two thrusting pelvises facing each other (42).

But they are also two heads facing each other (43), one menacing, the other somewhat recoiling. And they are also two rocks in the desert. To isolate, as one has been doing, some of Moore's recurrent associative images is beside the point. The point is, of course, that the forms are several images, are metamorphic, suggest correspondences between different things. If there is one constant which distinguishes Moore's language of ambiguous biomorphic forms from those of his contemporaries, it probably lies in the coincidence of landscape with oral and genital references. The human body becomes at the same time its own most secret parts and a part of its elementary environment.

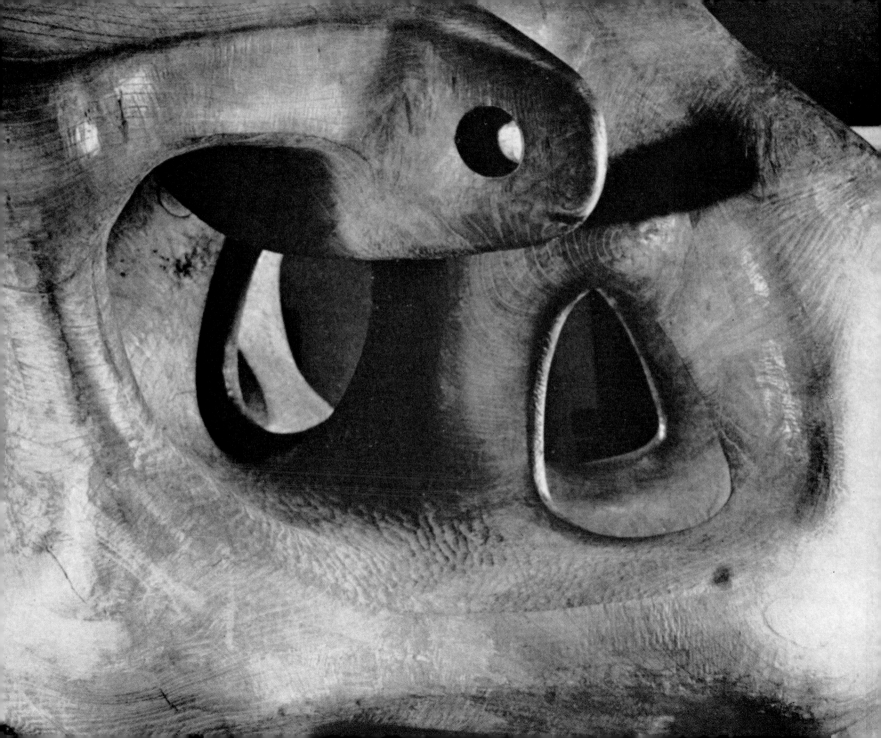

31 Composition 1931, height 19 in.

32 Figure 1933–4, height 30 in.

33 Composition 1932, height 17½ in.

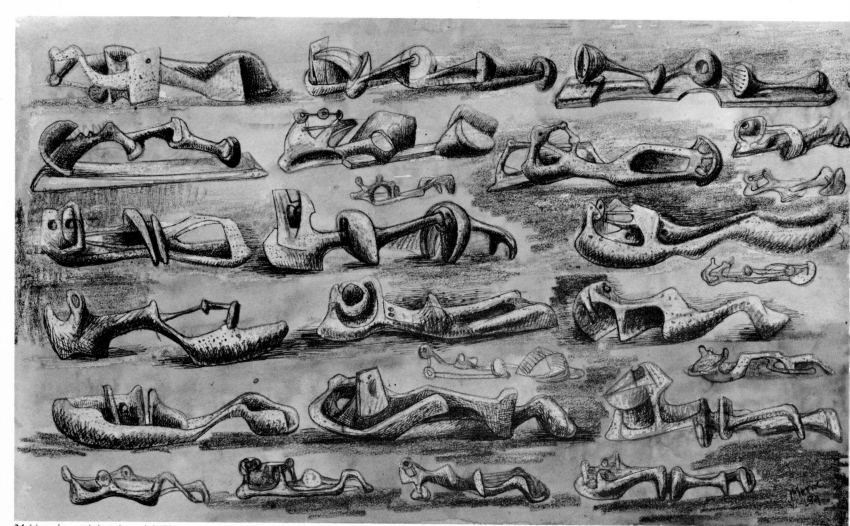

34 Ideas for sculpture in metal 1939

35 Reclining figure 1938, length 13 in.

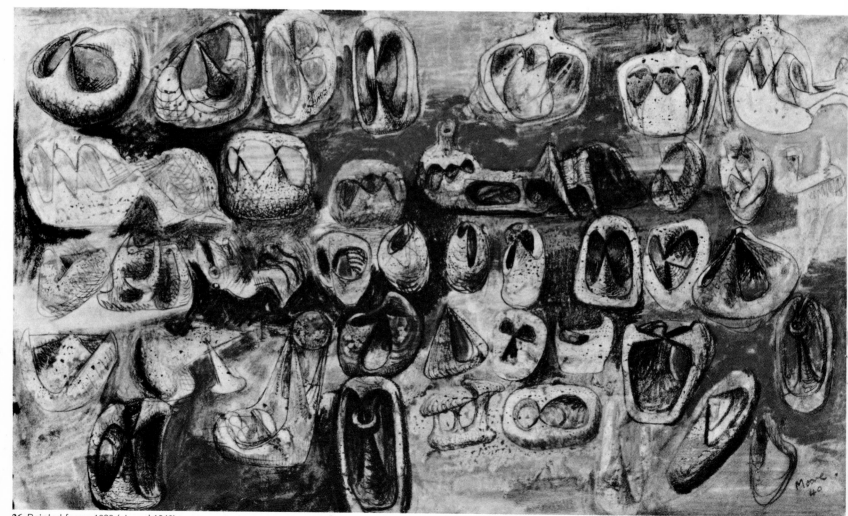

36 Pointed forms 1939 (signed 1940)

37 Three points 1939, length 7½ in.

38 Three rings 1966, length 39 in.

39 Three rings 1966, length 39 in.

40 Three-piece reclining figure No.1 1961–2, length 113 in.

1 Three-piece reclining figure No.1 1961–2, length 113 in.

42 Two forms 1966–7, length 60 in.

51

43 Two forms 1966–7, length 60 in. (detail)

Stones, Bones, Shells

About 1928–9 Moore began to make a habit of examining and collecting pebbles and shells and bones. His sketch-books of the early 30s included several sheets of studies of bones (46) and a few of shells (45). In 1932 he used a pebble, one with a hole through it, as a beginning for a sculpture, building onto it in concrete to form a *Mother and Child*. In 1934 he made some small biomorphic abstract sculptures by working on found pebbles. He had already, in 1930, carved four iron-stone pebbles into pieces of figurative sculpture, but there he had treated the pebbles simply as raw material like any other pieces of stone. In 1934, on the other hand, he did no more than modify the pebbles' shapes, so that it is impossible to judge from the finished sculpture (47) how far the form was found, how far imposed. He carved a hole through the pebble in one case, but the hole might equally well have been present in the pebble as found. After this, nearly twenty years passed before Moore again worked so directly on or from natural objects as in these sculptures and the sketch-book drawings. In the meantime, however, he looked at them closely and constantly, and sought to put into his work the 'principles of form and rhythm'[1] which he found in them.

'Pebbles and rocks show nature's way of working stone. Smooth, sea-worn pebbles show the wearing away, rubbed treatment of stone and principles of asymmetry.'[2] For a couple of years on either side of the time of writing, 1933–4, Moore's stone-carvings generally reflect the study of 'smooth, sea-worn pebbles' but still tend to differ from the pieces which actually began as pebbles by having a sharp edge somewhere to contrast with the smoothly modulated curves that might have been shaped by the sea (5, 62, 64). From 1936 the sharp edges multiplied so that the carvings became more angular than curvilinear (6, 53), with some exceptions (8).

'Rocks show the hacked, hewn treatment of stone, and have a jagged nervous block rhythm.' At the time, Moore made only one small piece with this 'jagged nervous block rhythm'. It was not until 1959 onwards, in his series of two-piece reclining figures, that he made much of the idea of imitating rocks (11, 41). And then the 'hacked, hewn treatment' was applied not to stone, but to a more tractable material: plaster (made permanent in bronze). In 1934 Moore was implying that the 'principles of form and rhythm' discovered in a given kind of natural object could show the sculptor how to work a kindred material (e.g., forms found in pebbles were appropriate for stone-carvings but not wood-carvings). By the time he got around to doing rock-like sculptures, he no longer felt committed to the doctrine of 'truth to material', felt the same sort of licence to make rocks in bronze as Rodin to make bronzes with unfinished passages resembling those in Michelangelo's marbles.

'Bones have marvellous structural strength and hard tenseness of form, subtle transition of one shape into the next and great variety in section.' Here Moore makes no connexion with a particular medium. The earliest pieces which seem to reflect observation of bones were carvings in wood – a *Composition* of 1933 in walnut and the *Two Forms* of 1934 in Pynkado wood where the shapes around the entrance to the hollow form (136) might have been based on some of the studies of bones in the sketch-books. But obviously the one medium into which most bone-forms could readily be translated was metal, which Moore began using constantly in 1939. The first of the series of small reclining figures modelled in wax and cast in lead was that (35) in which the legs are replaced by one bone-like shape. Thereafter he could have had bones in mind when creating certain rather linear metal inventions, both reclining (10) and standing.

'Trees (tree trunks) show principles of growth and strength of joints, with easy passing of one section into the next. They give the ideal for wood sculpture, upward twisting movement.' This was a clear affirmation of the doctrine of truth to material. In fact, Moore's wood-carvings of the 1930s, though freer and more open than those in stone, do not in the main possess an essentially different kind of rhythm: the two elm reclining figures carved in 1936 have the same sort of shapes and articulation as the Hornton stone recliner of 1938 (8). But the elm recliner of 1939 (68) beautifully embodies the 'twisting movement' which was the ideal. (Presumably he was envisaging only upright sculpture when he talked about 'upward twisting movement', actually meant movement along the length of a wood-carving, whether this was standing up or lying down.)

'Shells show nature's hard but hollow form (metal sculpture) and have a wonderful completeness of single shape.' The sort of sculpture Moore had in mind emerged towards the end of his first year of working constantly in metal. This was in the first of his works comprising an interior and an exterior piece, *The Helmet* (77, 78), and a related *Figure* which has no interior piece. But 'helmet' is exact, and both these objects seem more like armour than like shells, as do the 'helmet heads' of the early 1950s. One major piece of the latter period, the *Reclining figure (external form)* of 1953–4 (73), does seem to reflect the influence of shells. What Moore could not conceive of in 1934 was that he would at some time overcome the technical problem of carving marble into forms resembling shells, as he did thirty years later in the two versions of *Three Rings* (38, 74). Here the issue of truth to material is not involved. Clearly the connexion made in 1934 between shell forms and metal sculpture was purely practical, the question being how hollow the forms could manage to be in a given material, not how hollow they ought to be. Marble, indeed, is the more appropriate medium for forms like shells, because of its translucence.

In that article of 1934, Moore was mostly enunciating notions which had been explicit in an earlier, shorter, statement, published in 1930:[3] truth to material; direct carving; the rightness of hardness; full three-dimensionality; making masses work in opposition; energy pent-up in static forms; asymmetry; organic growth; the variety of nature; the autonomous vitality of the work of art; preference for power over beauty; the irrelevance of the classical and the Renaissance. There were just two new elements in the later text, each corresponding to one of the two important things that had happened in the meantime in his work – the growth of his concern with natural objects, and that his style had gone abstract. So in 1930 he writes that the sculptor's inspiration 'will come, as always, from nature and the world around him, from which he learns such principles as balance, rhythm, organic growth of life, attraction and repulsion, harmony and contrast', whereas in 1934 these universals give way to the account of the concrete lessons to be learned from the study of stones and bones. On the subject of abstraction, in 1930 he says that art which is, 'as Music and Architecture are, non-representational', is one of the currently valid possibilities: in 1934, having to some degree embraced that possibility, he speaks of the importance to himself of 'abstract qualities', goes on to say that for him the 'psychological human element' is no less important, and later concludes his article with the plea that art which 'does not aim at reproducing natural appearances' is not therefore escapist, decorative or sedative but 'may be a penetration into reality . . . an expression of the significance of life'. His next published statement, three years later, was to end in exactly the same way: 'My sculpture is becoming . . . what some people would call more abstract; but only because I believe that in this way I can present the human psychological content of my work with the greatest directness and intensity.'[4] He was painfully anxious to allay any suspicion that his abstract direction meant a retreat from reality. Certainly, his defensiveness must have been aroused by the violent abuse that had been showered on his work. Moreover, he may have wanted to make it clear how his position differed from that of close associates such as Ben Nicholson.[5] Nevertheless, he protests like a man conducting an argument with himself.

There may have been a connexion between his need to reassure himself that abstraction was not an escape from reality and his preoccupation with stones and bones and shells. Obviously, these natural objects could be valuable models for, or elements in, a biomorphic abstract sculptural language, both formally and iconographically: formally, because they are both organic and hard, and sculpture is hard, and Moore wanted his sculpture to look organic, and hard; iconographically, because of their potential for evoking things other than themselves, so that shapes derived from them could have a mysterious ambiguity. But perhaps Moore's faith in their value was enhanced by a need to ell himself that his abstract forms were obeying some authority beyond that of his own instincts, were therefore nor arbitrary, not products of personal taste or fantasy, but were sanctioned by nature, did not merely represent his preferences, his decisions, his way of working stone'. It is Picasso's entire confidence in his own instincts, his own gestures, his own power to confer life and meaning on whatever he cares to use, that makes him exploit that vast and capricious range of found objects, natural, man-made, beaten-up, brand new – whether in actuality or, as in *An Anatomy* (157), illusionistically. Moore limits his choice to objects which he feels he can depend on as having an intrinsic meaning and virtue. But why is it that the pebble, and other hard organic objects of a similar size, should have such a special value? In 1937 Moore wrote that the sculptor 'must strive continually to think of, and use, form in its full spatial completeness. He gets the solid shape, as it were, inside his head – he thinks of it, whatever its size, as if he were holding it completely enclosed in the hollow of his hand.'[6] And lately he has said: 'I prefer to do a sketch-model a hand-size that you can turn around and control, as though you're God.'[7] Perhaps it is because these natural objects are things that can be enclosed within the sculptor's hand, known by the sculptor's hand, that they seem to Moore to offer a way, 'a penetration into reality' – that they can be trusted.

He has trusted them still more in some ways since the mid-50s. Until then, Moore's customary process of crystallizing ideas for sculptures had been by drawing – drawing 'as a means of generating ideas for sculpture,

tapping oneself for the initial idea'[8] – and then selecting the most promising designs for realization in the round – until about 1935 by direct carving of the definitive work, since then by first making a sketch-model (or several) and basing the definitive work on this (or one of them). (Sometimes, with very large works, there has been an intermediate version, used as the working model for the biggest version.) Since the mid-50s Moore has almost eliminated drawing from the process, has used the improvising of sketch-models as the initial stage, so that from the outset the image has multiple points of view. And a high proportion of the sketch models have had as their point of departure a found stone or bone or fragment of bone, while others have been made up while looking at stones and bones – as well, of course, as while remembering them. From the start of this period, the found objects themselves have been quite different in character from those which influenced Moore in the 30s and 40s. The stones are now rarely the 'smooth, sea-worn pebbles' which showed 'the wearing away, rubbed treatment of stone'. They are mostly stones found inland – flints with sharply undulating contours and corners broken off leaving a jagged facet (48). The bones are often fragments, cut through by the butcher's saw (and found buried in a part of Moore's garden where a butcher's shop existed centuries ago). The objects are altogether rougher, more irregular, than before.

The *Warrior with Shield* originated in the piece of stone which became the stump of a leg and a hip in the sketch-model (49). A *Seated Torso* began as the flint which is the head and neck and armless shoulder of the

sketch-model (48). The torso of the *Two-Piece Reclining Figure: Lincoln Centre* (89) was developed from a bone. The head end of the *Three-Piece Reclining Figure No. 2: Bridge Prop* (50) was based upon a bone. The head and neck of *Seated Woman: Thin Neck* was a bone, and this neck inspired the *Standing Figure: Knife-Edge* (113). In the *Three Motives against Wall No.2* (52), the piece on the right is an altered copy of a stone; the other pieces are invented forms reminiscent of stones. *Three-Way Piece: Points* (44) was inspired by a stone fragment with three points touching the ground. The *Working Model for Locking Piece* (129) (there was no sketch-model) was based on the accidental locking together of two stones and on the way two bones joined together. *Slow Form: Tortoise* (128) was made of five modified duplicates of part of a stone. Some of the preliminary sketch-models for the wall relief for the Rotterdam Bouwcentrum (116) were composed by making an impression in clay of stones, shells, metal objects – manufactured things, for once – and old sketch-models of Moore's,[9] then taking plaster casts from these negatives. The definitive model (51) looks like a group of shells and fossils embedded in the sand. The very recent *Two-Piece Sculpture No. 11* (135, 137) and *Three-Piece Sculpture: Vertebrae* (140) are made of invented forms built up while looking at and handling bones and stones. Instead of more or less automatic drawing, the hand moving freely over a page, Moore's unordered point of departure now is to use his hands on something they can get hold of.

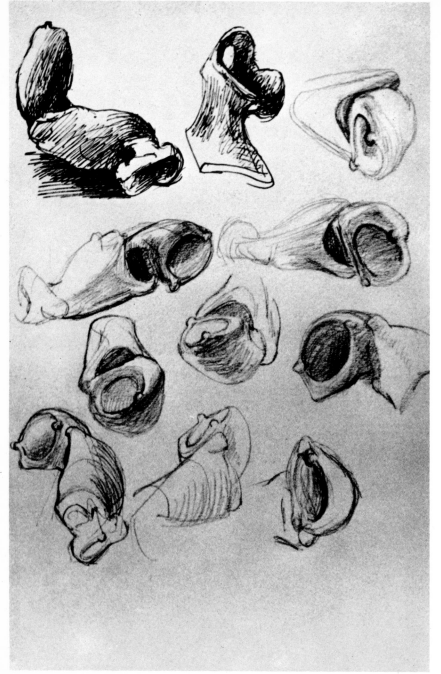

45 Studies of a lobster claw and a bone 1932

46 Studies of bones 1932

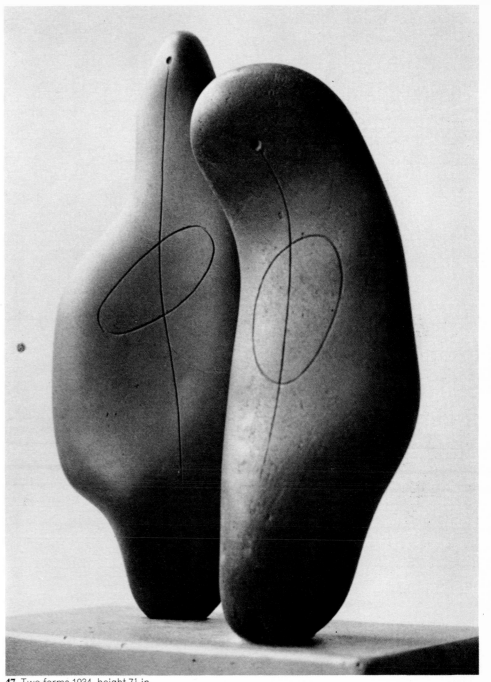

47 Two forms 1934, height 7¼ in.

48 Sketch-model for Seated torso 1954, height 5½ in.

49 Sketch-model for Warrior with shield 1952–3, height 7¾ in.

50 Three-piece reclining figure No. 2: Bridge prop 1963, length 99 in.

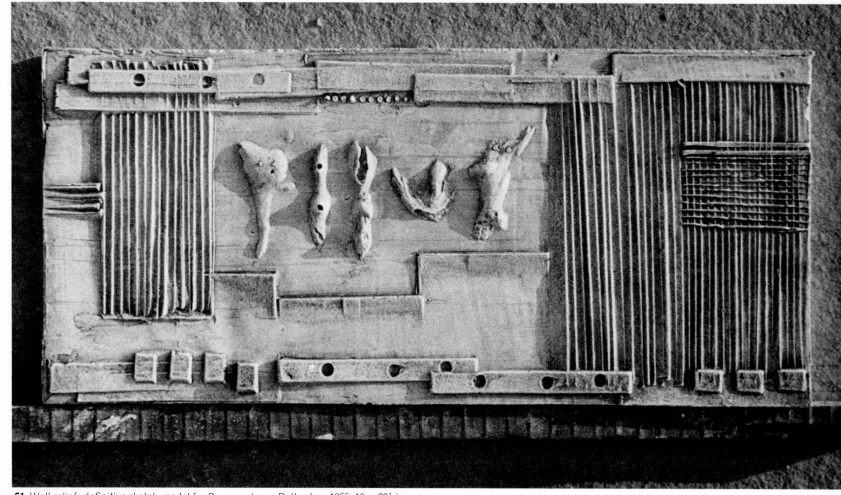

51 Wall relief: definitive sketch-model for Bouwcentrum, Rotterdam 1955, 10 × 22½ in.

52. Three motives against wall No.2 1959, length 42¼ in.

Square Form

A certain squareness of form has been a common attribute of twentieth-century carving from the time of Picasso's wood *Figure* of 1907, Derain's stone *Crouching Man* of 1907, and Brancusi's various versions of *The Kiss*. It has been motivated by the notion of respecting the material, therefore the block, by seeing power rather than elegance as the ideal, by rejecting the Greek tradition in favour of the Egyptian, the Sumerian, the Mexican. It characterizes most of Moore's finest carvings of the 1920s and even imposes itself at this time on drawings from life (57). Egyptian block-statues were one of his models at the outset (16), but the key influence was, of course, the Mexican, especially Teotihuacán, Toltec and Aztec (54, 58).

At the same time, the symmetry which is a concomitant of squareness in primitive and archaic art is rejected. For example, the head of the *Chacmool* from Chichén Itzá (144) typically has matching protuberances on either side, whereas the head of Moore's first variation on it (54) has a large protuberance on one side, none on the other – a configuration which recurs in his heads of all periods. The projection seems to be a schematic rendering of gathered hair – a sort of cubic bun – only, adjacent distortions suggest, not as if this were a representation of an asymmetric coiffure, but as if part of the

back of the head had been wrenched round to one side. There are also heads (1) in which the hair is not treated in this way but there is a dislocation of one of the head's lateral planes. An analogous device sometimes appears in Moore's drawings (57): a face combines frontal and profile views as if a lateral plane had been brought into the frontal. This sort of conjunction of views frequently occurs in Picasso heads from the mid-20s on. But it is also to be found in the head of the Virgin in the Michelangelo cartoon in the British Museum. Moore cannot remember whether he noticed it there before seeing double heads by Picasso. In any case, the idea of moving part of a plane around into one at right-angles to it – the back of a head to the side, the side to the front – is a cubist way of conveying a sense of volume.

The squareness recurs in abstract inventions of the mid-1930s, mostly carvings in stone (53, 60, 62, 64) and drawings as if of stone objects (55, 59). Two abstract heads in Hornton stone of 1936, each entitled *Square Form* (53), recall certain Mexican images of animals and birds, such as the Toltec macaw. The linear incisions in the surface of one of these – and in several other stone-carvings of the time – clearly relate to current geometric abstract painting. In another abstract head of the same year, *Carving* in Travertine marble,

a flat plane treated as a bas-relief – with three recessed circles, a projecting right-angled shape and incised straight lines – seems inspired by Ben Nicholson's recent *White Reliefs* (actually, the right-angled bit was suggested by L-plates on cars). The volumes, on the other hand, are strongly organic in feeling. Despite the wide currency of squareish form in modern sculpture, the squareish biomorph is Moore's personal convention – like the stringed figure (14, 93, 94, 95) (which also combines biomorphic masses with straight lines), an entirely personal contribution to the idioms of abstract Surrealism.

54 Reclining figure 1929, length 33 in.

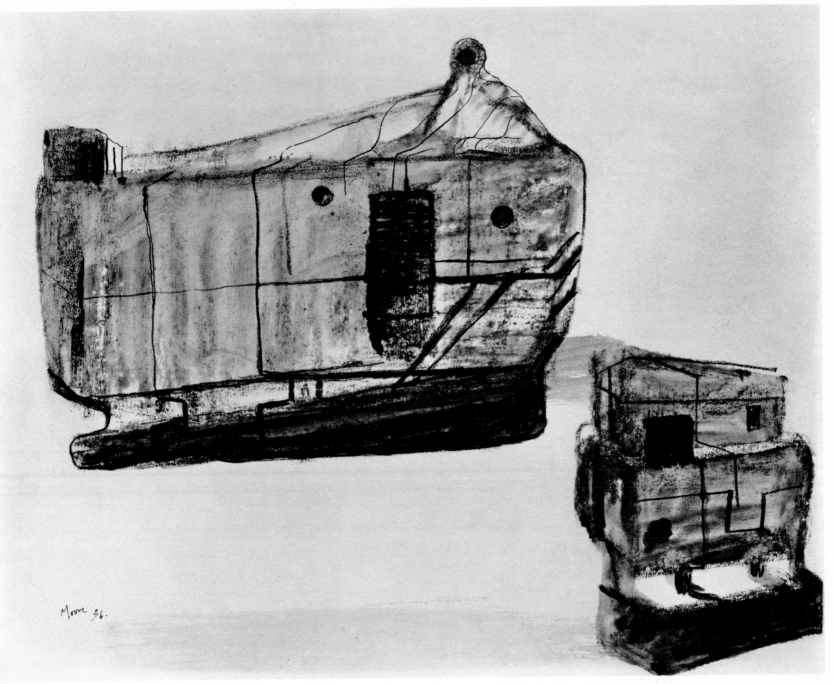

55 Drawing 1936

56 Drawing from life: seated figure *c.* 1933–4 (signed 1933)

57 Drawing from life: seated figure 1928

58 Figure with clasped hands 1929, height 16¾ in.

59 Stones in landscape 1936

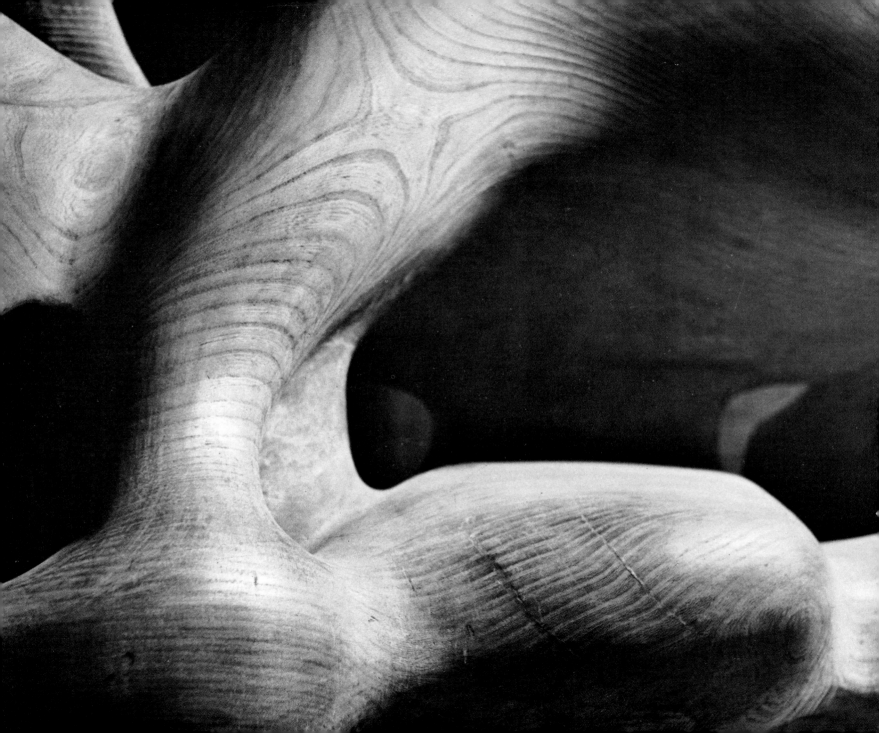

Holes and Hollows

When Moore did a carving in 1924–5 of *Two Heads* in Mansfield stone, his idea was that, whereas a single head gave a compact volume, carving a pair of heads from one block would entail driving a space between them, penetrating the block. Believing that a sculpture cannot be really three-dimensional in feeling unless the intactness of the block has been broken down, Moore has gone on finding subjects and poses which give a pretext for letting space into the composition. But of course he has also, like other twentieth-century artists, made sculptures with spaces let in arbitrarily, whether as holes piercing a form – as in the head and the torso of Archipenko's terracotta *Walking Woman* of 1912 (162), in Brancusi's carved oak *Chimera* of 1918 (161), etc. – or whether by hollowing-out a mass so that a convex surface is replaced by a concave – as in the legs of the same Archipenko, in Boccioni's bronze *Development of a Bottle in Space* of 1912, in Picasso's polychromed bronze *Glass of Absinthe* of 1914 (160), in Gabo's sheet iron *Head* of 1916 etc. These devices have mostly been used in modelled or constructed, rather than carved, sculpture, and Moore's first tentative arbitrary holes and hollows – apart from the hole in place of an eye piercing the profile *Head* in slate of 1930 (107) – occurred in modelled sculptures – the hollow in a concrete *Half-figure* of 1929 and a lead *Reclining Figure* of 1931, the hole in a concrete *Mother and Child* of 1932 built around a found pebble with a hole through it. Moore came to use holes and hollows with more freedom, naturally enough, as his language became more abstract – in carvings (32) and drawings for sculpture (67) of 1933. By 1934 he had made sculptures in which form is opened out in an alternative way, by dividing a figure into parts (83, 86) and a sculpture foreshadowing the creation of hollow forms with a form inside them (63). These two concepts were not fully developed till later. But the penetration of the figure by holes and hollows became a central preoccupation from now on. The first excavated figures were the two elm recliners of 1936; their great successor of 1939 (7, 68) has remained the most extremely opened-out of Moore's wood-carvings. Oddly enough, he has produced only one major opened-out reclining figure in stone (8): it is perhaps the finest of all his carvings. Only in certain marbles of the 60s has he made stone-carvings (74) as open as his most open wood-carvings, but these have so far not been whole figures. The most extremely spatial sculptures have naturally, for technical reasons been in metal (10, 71), – This from the time of some of the statuettes modelled in wax in 1939.

In the statement he published in 1937, Moore repeated something said in 1934, 'Pebbles show nature's way of working stone'[1] but this time added: 'Some of the pebbles I pick up have holes right through them'.[2] From there he went on to talk about holes in sculpture. The intended implication, presumably, was that when he carved a hole through a sculpture, he was working stone as nature does. The imagery is governed by a fantasy of erosion. 'The mystery of the hole' in a sculpture is 'the mysterious fascination of caves in hillsides and cliffs'.[3] Occasionally it is the mystery of the eye-sockets in a skull (69) – where again nature has eaten something away – or that of cave and skull simultaneously (66); once, sudden damage seems to have been inflicted, where a head is as if pitted with bullet-holes (65).[4] But the image which is peculiarly Moore's is that of a tunnel or cavern, dramatically dark and light, which can be entered in imagination (61, 68, 70). If it also evokes the interior of a woman's body, it is not so much in regard to the idea of sexual penetration as to that of being wholly inside it. The image of the cavernous reclining figure subsumes that of the mother and child.

61 Reclining figure 1945–6, length 75 in. (detail)

62 Three forms 1934, height 16 in.

63 Two forms 1934, length 21 in.

64 Four forms 1936, length 22 in.

65 Head 1937, height 21 in.

66 Armless seated figure against round wall 1957, height 11 in.

67 Drawing for sculpture 1933

68 Reclining figure 1939, length 8

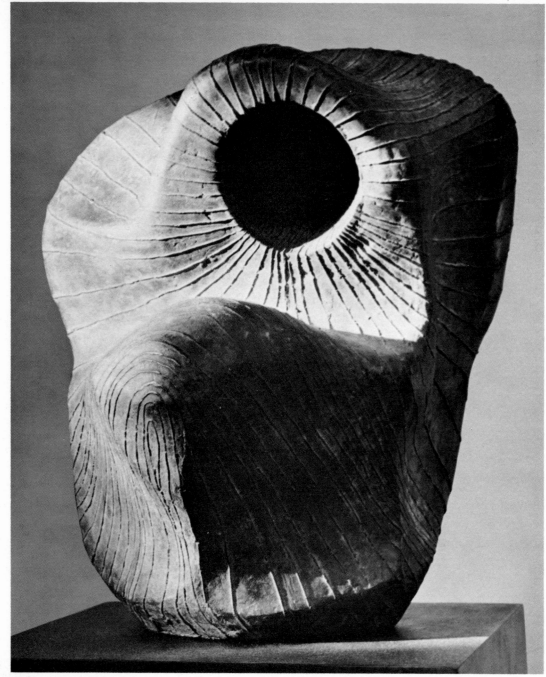

69 Head: Lines 1955, height 11¾ in.

70 Reclining figure 1945–6, length 75 in. (de

71 Reclining figure 1939, length 10¼ in.

72 Reclining figure 1939, length 10¼ in.

73 Reclining figure (external form) 1953–4, length 84 in.

4 Three rings 1966–7, length 106 in.

Internal/External

Moore began making sculptures consisting of two or three or four separate pieces in 1934. In one of the first of these compositions (26), a large hollow form looms like a hood over a small compact form, as if protecting it and threatening to devour it. It's a decidedly maternal image, and it suggests the possibility of sculpture in which a form is enclosed within a hollow shell with an opening or openings through which the internal form is visible. Moore's first sculpture of this kind, *The Helmet* (77, 78), was one of the last things he made before he stopped doing sculpture in 1940; drawings of 1939–40 show that he had several other such ideas in mind – some in which the external form is again a hollow head (76), others in which it is a full-length figure. The concept reappears in sketch-book pages of 1947–8, and in 1950 Moore realized some more *Helmets*. During the next four years he made versions in different sizes of a standing figure and a reclining figure with internal forms, though in the final version of the reclining piece the internal form was eliminated, leaving an empty shell (73). He has since made several minor works with internal and external forms, and one major masterpiece, the *Reclining Mother and Child* of 1960–1 (25, 75, 79, 80).

Here the child for which there often seems to be a place in the reclining figures is finally present. The form it assumes suggests the common infantile fantasy of associating babies inside women's bodies with penises inside women's bodies. To be precise, it is reminiscent of a horse's genitals. At the same time, the tail end of the external form, from certain angles (80), has the particular shape of a horse's rump, so that one of the images evoked is of a horse fallen on its side. Seen through one of the two windows in the back (75), the internal form suggests a foreshortened view of the neck and shoulders of a decapitated man. Even apart from any such specific associations, the child-form is powerfully ambiguous – at once explosively aggressive and a blunt huddled baby animal. The mother appears from the front to be nursing it, retaining it, from the back to be giving birth, expelling it. The profoundest contradiction lies beyond any specific images evoked: it is the simultaneous embodiment in the concave of the woman's body of springy muscularity and enveloping protectiveness. Energy and tenderness become one, as in sexual passion.

The inclusion of a child within a reclining woman is suggested in an earlier major work, the elm *Reclining Figure* of 1945–6 (81, 82). Its torso is partly a mysterious slotted form, contained by the breasts jutting out above it and the cradling arm, which is like a separate entity burrowing into the body. In the previous large elm, the breasts have the form of reptilean heads (30); here the diaphragm is like a head with a rapacious mouth. Or, rather, the shape is both something that is eating into the chest and the chest itself partially eaten away. Moore's intention was that the slotted form should suggest a palpitating heart. That is to say, he saw it as an internal organ, so that in any case the figure is of the family of those combining internal and external forms.

75 Reclining mother and child 1960–1, length 86½ in.

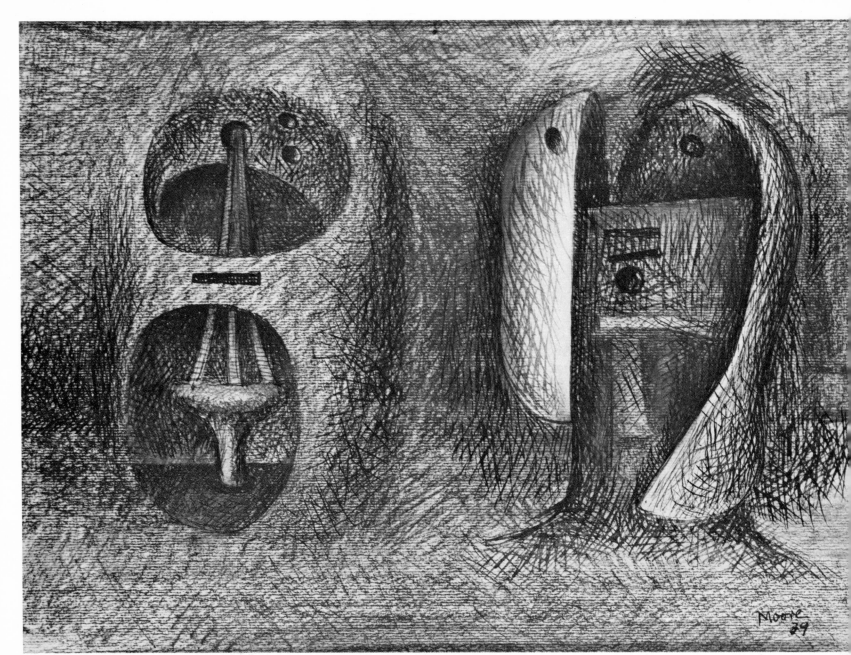

76 Two heads: drawing for metal sculpture 1939

The helmet 1939, height 11½ in.

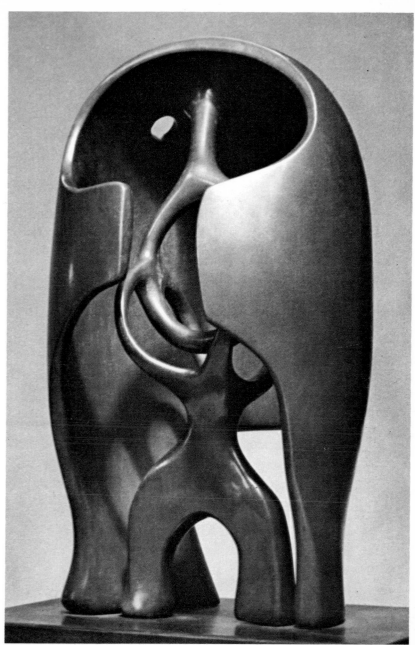

78 The helmet 1939, height 11½ in.

79 Reclining mother and child 1960–1, length 86½ in.

0 Reclining mother and child 1960–1, length 86½ in.

81 Reclining figure 1945–6, length 75 in.

82 Reclining figure 1945–6, length 75 in. (detail)

Divided Figures

Among the 1934 sculptures made up of separate forms are two four-piece compositions that are not simply compositions but reclining figures taken apart. The first (83) was made in reinforced concrete, much later cast in bronze, the second (86) carved in Cumberland alabaster. A drawing of 1933 (85) anticipates both in one way or another, while more obviously remaining a reclining figure than either sculpture does. (Another drawing, of 1934, was the actual study for the carving.)

Moore may have got the idea of sculptures in separate parts from compositions by Arp (163) or Giacometti (164) made about three years earlier (and meanwhile reproduced in *Cahiers d'Art*). But if there was a source for the idea of dividing up a figure into parts, this was probably certain Picasso paintings and drawings of around 1930 (165): certainly, the bone-like forms of these Picassos are recalled by the carved four-piece recliner. The concrete version recalls in its angularity a Giacometti sculpture, the *Slaughtered Woman* of 1932 (166), which is not in separate parts but is a reclining figure spread out as if all but dismembered and resembling a dead insect or arachnid.

Twenty-five years later, Moore started dividing the reclining figure again, at first into two parts. There always had been a tendency for the head end and leg end of the recliners to have opposing rhythms, and in the figure for the forecourt of the UNESCO building (sketch-model, 1956; working model, 1957; final carving 1957–8), the extreme *contrapposto* almost detached the two ends. The next large recliner he made became the *Two-Piece Reclining Figure No. 1* of 1959 (11, 87, 88, 90), though the sketch-model for it was in one piece: the decision to divide the figure was made in the course of working on the full-scale version. One reason for it was that Moore 'realized what an advantage a separated two-piece composition could have in relating figures to landscape. Knees and breasts are mountains. Once these two parts become separated you don't expect it to be a naturalistic figure; therefore, you can more justifiably make it like a landscape or a rock.'[1]

The figure can also be two figures. In the *Two-Piece Reclining Figure No. 1* there are some angles – and no other work of Moore's reads so differently from different angles – from which the parts seem to face each other like creatures in a stately mating dance (11). The rearing leg can also be the wing of a great swan, and one is suddenly reminded of the confrontation between Zeus and Leda. As if the symbolism of the myth were not already phallic enough, here the entire looming form can be equated with a threatening phallus (90). In the *Two-Piece Reclining Figure: Lincoln Center* (89), the roles played by the two parts are reversed: here the head end is rampant and domineering like a crowing cockerel. At the same time there is a contrary suggestion of a mother-and-child relationship like that of the Pynkado wood *Two Forms* of 1934 (26). The relationship within the *Two-Piece Reclining Figure No. 2* is asexual, purely aggressive. But on the whole this series presents by far the most specifically sexual imagery in Moore's work (specifically sexual as the cavernous figures are not). Where there is no total equation of one part of the figure with a phallus, the torso part is likely to have a phallic appendage directed at the lower part (12, 84). The appendage may in the first place be a truncated thigh. But there is one drawing of 1961 of a two-piece figure in which the lower half is a huge mouth opened wide to receive an inexplicable elongated form sticking out of the torso. The connotations are not intended – a likely reason for their power.

'The two-piece sculptures pose a problem of relationship: the kind of relationship between two people. It's very different once you divide a thing into three.'[2] Wanting this, Moore did several try-outs, of which he cast only one in bronze (91), before having an idea he chose to realize, in 1961–2, on a large scale (40, 41). 'What led me to this solution

83 Composition 1934, length 17½ in.

was finding a little piece of bone that was the middle of a backbone, and I realized then that perhaps the connexion was through one piece to another – one could have gone on and made a four- or five-piece, like a snake carrying through with its vertebrae.'[3]

The first of the big three-piece recliners has the same rugged, jagged, scored, rock-like forms as the seven big two-piece recliners made between 1959 and the mid-60s. The second big three-piece figure, made in 1963 and called *Bridge Prop* (50, 132), has clean-cut forms, virtually smooth surfaces, and is neither rock-like nor in any other way landscapeish. The head end is decidedly organic – indeed, is based upon a bone – and the leg end is somewhat so, but the middle form looks man-made, architectonic – a bridge between the ends that is arched like a bridge, and a prop for the head end, which leans upon it, clasps it at two points so that they fit together.

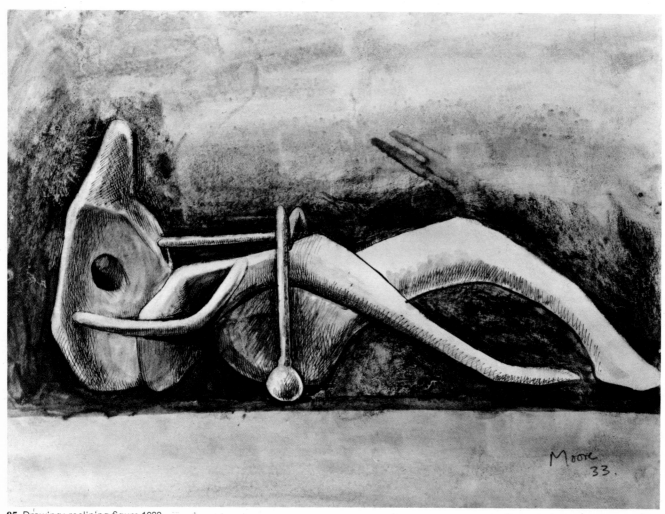

85 Drawing: reclining figure 1933

86 Four-piece composition: reclining figure 1934, length 20 in.

87 Two-piece reclining figure No.1 1959, length 76 in.

88 Two-piece reclining figure No.1 1959, length 76 in.

89 Working model for Two-piece reclining figure: Lincoln Center 1963, length 14 ft.

90 Two-piece reclining figure No.1 1959, length 76 in.

91 Three-piece reclining figure: sketch-model No.1 1961, length 7¾ in.

92 Three-piece reclining figure: sketch-model No.2: Polished 1962, length 8½ in.

Strings

The idea of making stringed sculptures was derived from certain models in the Science Museum, illustrating mathematical propositions (168), which had first impressed Moore in his student days. The first stringed sculptures were a relief and an upright form carved in wood in 1937. Three more were carved in wood in 1938 – two of them abstract, the other a head – and one in 1939, *Bird Basket* (94), the most complex of the stringed sculptures. In 1939, several were modelled in wax and cast in lead, with wire added as against the string of the wood-carvings: there were two treatments of the mother-and-child theme (14), a reclining figure, a composition (93) conceived as the detached head-and-shoulders of a reclining figure, an upright figure – an offspring of one of the carvings – called *The Bride* (95) (it is veiled by its strings and, beyond this veil, receptive), and a horizontal composition with rather similar forms. A few small pieces modelled in clay – some intended as sketch-models – in 1938–39 have since, at various times, been cast in lead or, mostly, bronze. Bronze editions have also been made of certain pieces initially cast in lead. Elastic string has been used for the late casts rather than wire, which had proved too vulnerable.

The introduction of the strings was a function of Moore's concern with making space within a sculpture a positive element. ('Sculpture in air is possible, where . . . the hole . . . is the intended and considered form'.[1]) The string creates a transparent barrier between the space enclosed within the concaves of the sculpture and the space around the sculpture. Movement of the eye along the length of the strings sharpens awareness of the space the sculpture encloses, especially when one set of strings can be seen through another, so that a counterpoint of movement is created which quickens the vibration of the space.

Nevertheless, the key factor is probably the physical contrast between the strings and the volumes. The volumes are solid and they are curvilinear; the strings are weightless and they are taut. They are straight lines, and their straightness speaks of necessity, not choice. They become symbols of precision. There is a general tendency in Moore's smooth metal sculptures of 1939 towards a mechanistic quality, something of the air and feel of a precision tool (37, 71, 78). The geometry of the strings intensifies that quality. The scale of the pieces confirms it: it is a scale that makes us relate these sculptures to our hands.

93 Stringed figure 1939, length 8½ in.

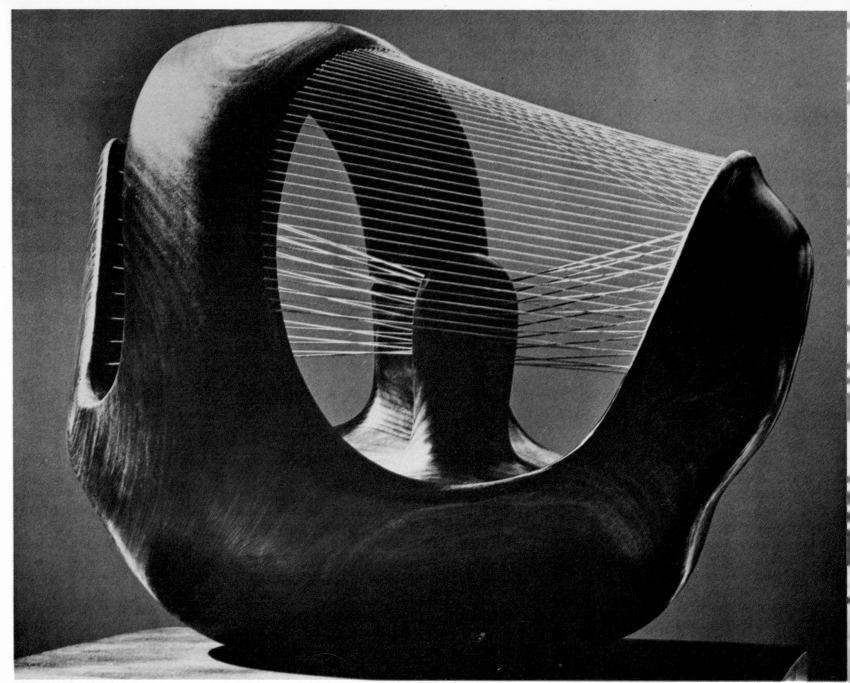

94 Bird basket 1939, length 16½ in.

95 The bride 1939, height 9⅜ in.

Draped

Drapery is the one recurrent element in Moore's sculpture which he never attempted in sculpture until he had used it exhaustively in drawings. There are perfunctory indications of drapery in various drawings of the early 1930s unrelated to sculpture. In 1938 Moore made a page of studies for an abandoned commission for some reliefs on the façade of Senate House, University of London. These are of a seated woman, and the last of them is draped in a style somewhat resembling the Northampton *Madonna* of 1943–4 (23). In 1939–40 Moore did a number of drawings with draped women, reclining, seated, standing, some holding a child: these include both studies for sculpture and drawings in their own right. One mixed sheet (97) – which is among some drawings (36) done in 1939 and mistakenly signed 'Moore 40' – contains several naturalistic draped figures and, in the top row, two reclining figures whose lower half is an opened-out barrel – as in one expressly metallic metal statuette of 1939 (71) – but also suggests heavy drapery. In 1940–1, observation of the shelterers wrapped in their blankets in the London Underground – impressions were recorded, always from memory, in sketch-books from which material was selected for elaboration into exhibition drawings (98, 99, 100) – developed Moore's use of drapery from a convention into a

powerful means of expression – more powerful, perhaps, than it has been since, in his drawings or sculpture. In 1942 Moore composed a large number of drawings with draped women, seated, standing, reclining, some of them sheets of separate figures, others pictures of figures grouped in imaginary settings. These drawings include the first studies for the *Three Standing Figures* to be carved in 1947–8 (from a sketch-model of 1945). Moore, then, crystallized several ideas for sculptures of draped figures in a fairly naturalistic idiom between 1938 and 1942.

The Northampton *Madonna* was followed by a stylistically similar draped reclining figure (96), commissioned as a memorial to be placed in the gardens of Dartington Hall. Moore carved it simultaneously with the big elm recliner of 1945–6 (81), the realization of another of the drawings made in 1942. 'I was working on both figures throughout a year. They are poles apart in feeling. But carving is a slow business, and if one works for too long a stretch upon a carving which satisfies only one side of one's nature, one becomes restive, one tends to become absorbed by projects which have not yet been started, and one's growing anxiety to be done with the thing one is working on will show in some of the forms. But if there is something with a quite different content on the go

at the same time there is an interplay of one's interests.'[1] While the figures were in progress, Moore was given to talking about them as representing opposing sides of his personality, the 'tough' and the 'tender', and he has talked ever since about his need, because of that opposition,[2] to work in antithetic styles concurrently, as he has.

It is not fortuitous that this polarization—as against the simple dichotomy of style present in 1931–2 and 1936[3] – began where it did, for it seems that Moore equates the use of drapery in sculpture with the expression of 'tender' to the exclusion of 'tough' feelings. This despite the fact that in the shelter drawings drapery plays a prominent part in some images that are positively apocalyptic (99). But it seems that in Moore's sculpture drapery is there to evoke certain kinds of art rather than life. In sculptures of the 40s (102, 103), it tends to evoke the Gothic. From the time of Moore's visit to Greece in 1951, it tends to evoke the classical (105). The little that he has added of his own has been to use the folds to create a variant of the metaphor of the figure as landscape, especially in one reclining figure (104) in which he sought 'to connect the contrast of the sizes of folds, here small, fine and delicate, in other places big and heavy, with the form of mountains, which are the crinkled skin of the earth'.[4]

96 Memorial figure 1945–6, length 56 in.

97 Drawing for sculpture 1939 (signed 1940)

98 Shelter scene: two swathed figures 1941

99 Shadowy shelter 1940

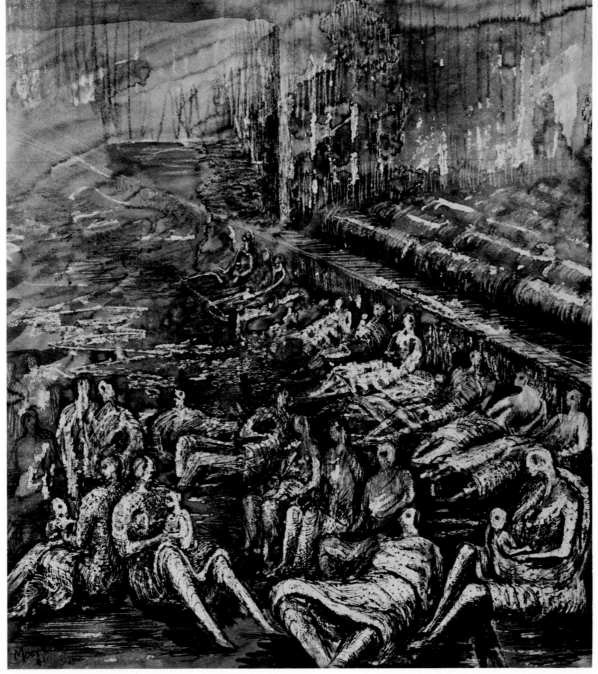

100 Tilbury shelter 1941

101 Sketch-model for Reclining figure No.4 1952, length 6¼ in.

115

2 Madonna and Child: sketch-model for Claydon Madonna 1943, height 7¼ in.

103 Sketch-model: Two seated women and a child 1945, height 6¾ in.

aped reclining figure 1952–3,
62 in. (detail)

105 Draped seated figure against curved wall 1956–7, height 9 in.

Knife-edge

In 1929–30, when his forms were generally bulky, Moore carved a few figures and heads from pieces of alabaster, ironstone or slate that were very slim in section (107). Certain drawings for metal sculpture of about 1937 have forms which could have been realized in sheet metal. In some of the small cast metal sculptures of 1939 there are forms which have a thinness in section doubtless inspired by shells (71) and bones. In 1942, after doing the last of the shelter drawings, Moore continued his service as an Official War Artist with drawings of miners at the coal-face. In these, his first studies since student days of the male nude, he represented the torso as a more or less flat, spade-like form (110). Two years later he started making sculptures of the male nude, in the sketch-models of family groups: in several of these, and in subsequent enlargements, the torso is treated as in the mine drawings. This flat, sharp-edged form has a rightness for metal sculpture and a rightness for conveying the energy and hardness of the male. But the same sort of form is used from 1950 in female figures (101), giving them a taut, alert, nervous look. In 1952 a variant appeared: instead of a torso with a convex back and a concave front, one with a convex front and a concave back, as in the *King and Queen* of 1952–3. This sculpture seems to me to look contrived and theatrical as an image, as well as impossibly inconsistent in its forms, but the backs of the two torsos (111), with their supple concave curve, are among the most beautiful passages in Moore's work.

In the 1960s the influence or incorporation of bones has produced semi-abstract figures with a flat torso (89), notably the *Standing Figure: Knife-edge* of 1961 (113), in which this form is tapered like a knife-blade, blunt along one edge, sharp along the other. In 1962 the knife-edge image was freed of this figure's allusion to bones, and made more vivid by perfectly smooth surfaces, as against a combination of smooth and rough, in the virtually abstract *Knife-Edge Two-Piece*. This was enlarged in 1965–6 into a version (112, 114) on a scale which makes it possible to walk through the narrow gap between the two pieces, as between two high walls: the forms are wedges cutting through space, and one advances through the passage like a wedge.

On a smaller scale, the *Moon head* of 1964 (108, 109) presents a similar parallel disposition of two flat forms with a narrow space between: one disc is a face, with characteristics of both profile and full face, the other a hand held up behind the head. The highly polished bronze gives rise, as one looks from the side through the gap between the discs, to a rippling effect in the facing inner surfaces, a ripple as of water which makes the blades seem altogether fluid, so that one feels that here too one is invited to penetrate the space.

In the *Sundial* of 1965–6 (106) the highly-polished knife-edge concept is used with exquisite logic in the design of a precision instrument. A mechanistic quality like that of the *Three Points* (37) and certain stringed figures (93, 95) of 1939 acquires a practical purpose.

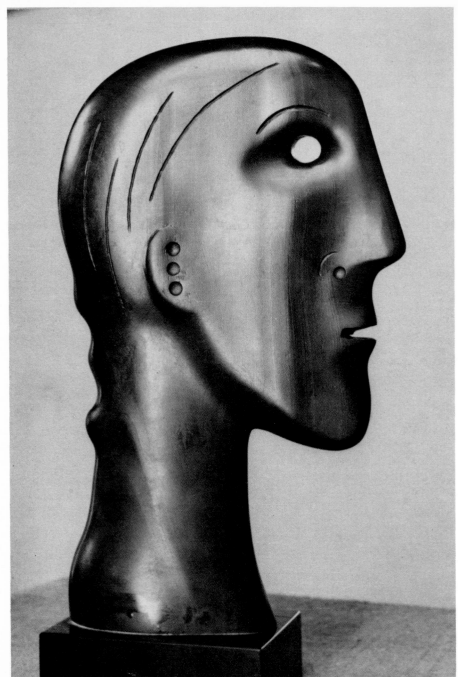

107 Head 1930, height 10 in.

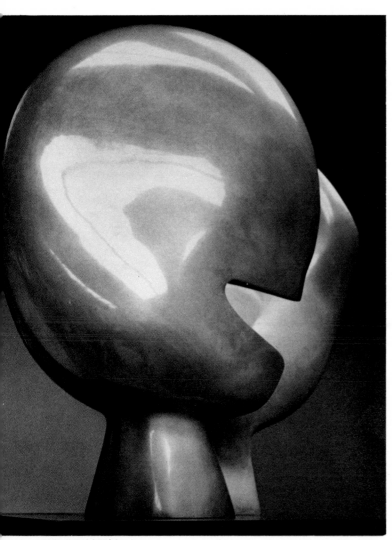

on head 1964, height 22½ in.

109 Moon head 1964, height 22½ in.

110 Studies of miners at work 1942 (detail)

111 King and Queen 1952–3, height 64½ in. (detail)

123

112 Knife-edge two-piece 1965, length 12 ft.

113 Standing figure: Knife-edge 1961, height 112 in.

114 Knife-edge two-piece 1965, length 12 ft.

Hard and Soft

In the sculptures carved or modelled before the 1950s, the notional surface tension is near enough equal all over. The surface appears uniformly firm; there are no parts which are distinctly softer than others. More recently, Moore has made a large number of sculptures in which there are violent contrasts of surface tension, with exceedingly taut, bone-hard, passages moving abruptly into soft, resilient, fleshy passages. This began at about the time when he started to work with stones that have partly smooth and partly rough surfaces and sudden alternations between convexes and concaves, rather than sea-worn pebbles with smooth surfaces and smooth curves.

Marked hard/soft contrasts first appeared in the early 1950s, in certain imaginary animal heads and a series of hand-size high reliefs of a mother and child. Their development became more systematic in the mid-50s, in some of the variant sketch-models for the wall reliefs designed for the Rotterdam Bouwcentrum (116) and then in some of the *Upright Motives* (118), where the kind of forms which are embedded in a ground in those reliefs become free-standing. The development of hard and soft in figurative sculpture was associated with the use of clinging quasi-classical drapery (105): whereas earlier draped figures (101, 102, 103) suggest no difference in surface tension between the clothes and the body, here drapery is soft, the body tauter. The first major sculpture of the nude in which the contrast is important was the bronze *Falling Warrior* of 1956–7 (120, 122). (In its predecessor by three years, the *Warrior with Shield*, the contrast is already there in one detail, the resilience of the thigh against the pointed hardness of the knee, but the torso is as uniformly hard as the flat torsos of previous male figures.) Since then, the hard/soft contrast has been a key characteristic of virtually all the clearly figurative bronzes (115, 119, 121) and of some of the more abstract ones: even the *Locking Piece* has soft passages (123).

Clearly, this new development was fostered by Moore's having come to work mainly in plaster – modelling followed by the carving of a relatively soft material. Rodin's influence is evident in the fluid, melting parts of the *Upright Motives*. But the crucial influence has been Michelangelo: indeed, the legs of the *Falling Warrior* are – what Moore suddenly recognized afterwards – a transposition of Christ's legs in the *Rondanini Pietà* (154). Only, he needed to be working in plaster to try and emulate the flexibility and the variation of tension which Michelangelo could get in carving marble. By the same token, his one early work that is somewhat Michelangelesque in idiom is the *Reclining Figure* of 1932 in carved reinforced concrete (3) – a medium in which he roughly modelled the form before he carved, was not carving an inhibitingly solid block. And this piece is not only much more flexibly and sharply articulated than any carving proper of the period, but gives some premonition of the hard/soft contrast. There are also certain drawings of the same year (117) in which hard and soft parts are related very much as in bronzes of twenty-odd years later. The idea of varying the surface tension was there from an early stage. Its realization was delayed, firstly by prohibitions which surrounded stone-carving – 'sculpture in stone should look honestly like stone'[1] – secondly by the persistence in the earlier works made in plaster of attitudes developed in working stone.

Now, Moore has at times used certain kinds of stone the texture and colour of which make the sculpture look altogether softer than is usual in his work. This happened in the mid-30s, in two carvings in Corsehill stone (5, 32). It has recurred in certain recent pieces in rosa aurora marble: whereas the red Soraya *Three Rings* (74) seem hard, the same shapes in rosa aurora (39) appear resilient. Again, after carving an *Upright Form Knife-edge* in rosa aurora, Moore found that the illusion of softness contradicted the hard character of the forms: for the first time in his

115 Headless animal 1959, length 9½ in.

career, he re-carved a piece in a different stone, a white marble. In these cases, however, the sense of softness does not alter the habitual consistency of surface tension.

On the other hand, the recent rosa aurora *Mother and Child* (28) does present a decided variation in surface tension, though a gradual variation without the abrupt contrasts of the bronzes. So too does a white marble *Reclining Form* of 1966. This, then, is a very new development in the stone-carvings, though it is somewhat foreshadowed in the torso of a Hornton stone *Reclining Figure* of 1949 in the collection of R. Sturgis Ingersoll. For obvious reasons the hard/soft contrast has been more readily developed in wood. There is a hint of it as far back as the Pynkado wood *Two Forms* of 1934 (136): the depths of the interior of the hollow form seem more resilient than the convex external surfaces. Then there is some suggestion of fleshy softness in the thighs of the 1945–6 elm recliner (81). And the next in the series, the one carved between 1959 and 1964 (9, 124, 125, 126) is richly varied in surface tension, with a sensuous elasticity in certain passages that is quite new in Moore's work.

The development of hard/soft contrasts represents a radically new way of thinking for Moore – an emphasis on dynamic rather than static qualities, and on the uneasy rather than the harmonious: it was no accident that the first characteristic hard-and-soft figure was the only figure he has ever made in sculpture with a totally off-balance, helpless pose (120)– helpless but violently, convulsively, energetic. 'One of the things I would like to think my sculpture has is a force, is a strength, is a life, a vitality from inside it, so that you have a sense that the form is pressing from inside trying to burst, or trying to give off the strength from inside itself, rather than having something which is just shaped from outside and stopped. It's as though you have something trying to make itself come to a shape from inside itself.'[2] This statement, made in the 60s, might so far be only an elaboration of Moore's old ideal of 'pent-up energy'[3] compressed in a work. But now he goes on: 'This is, perhaps, what makes me interested in bones as much as in flesh, because the bone is the inner structure of all living form. It's the bone that pushes out from inside; as you bend your leg the knee gets tautness over it, and it's there that the movement and the energy come from. If you clench a knuckle, you clench a fist, you get in that sense the bones, the knuckles, pushing through, giving a force that, if you open your hand and just have it relaxed, you don't feel. And so the knee, the shoulder, the skull, the forehead, the part where from inside you get a sense of pressure of the bone outwards – these for me are the key points.' What is new is the concern with 'key points' and 'pushing through'. In most of Moore's work the 'pent-up energy' underlies a surface the even tension of which implies that the energy is firmly contained, is not threatening to burst the bounds of the form. In the hard-and-soft works, passages where the surface is straining to contain something 'pressing from inside trying to burst' suddenly alternate with passages where the pressure is relaxed.

Underlying this new concern is a new extreme concentration on tactile and motor rather than visual sensations – on what is experienced in running one's hands over a body, responding more sharply to its hardnesses and softnesses, its hollows and bumps, than when looking at them, and on what is experienced in using one's own body, feeling one's skin stretching tautly over one's knuckles as one clenches a fist, feeling the muscles tighten as one extends a limb. The hard-and-soft figures are haptic images: they make bodies look the way they feel, from outside, and, still more perhaps, from inside. To the eye they can seem dislocated, awkward, uncouth. They ask to be looked through rather than looked at. In no other works has Moore taken such risks. And this reflects a further change of attitude – a growing acceptance, indeed, a positive courting, of imperfection, incompleteness.[4]

116 Wall relief: sketch-model No. 9 for Bouwcentrum relief, Rotterdam *c*. 1954–5, $13\frac{1}{2} \times 18\frac{1}{2}$ in

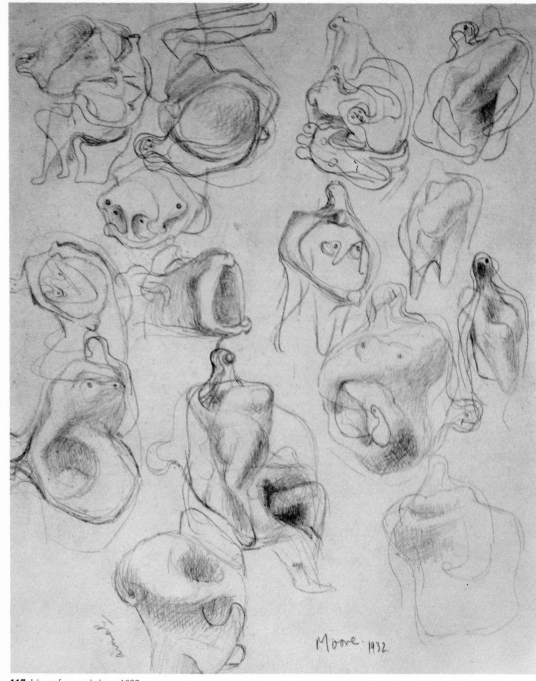

117 Ideas for sculpture 1932

118 Upright motives Nos.1, 2 and 7 1955–6, he
132 in., 126 in., 126 in. (de

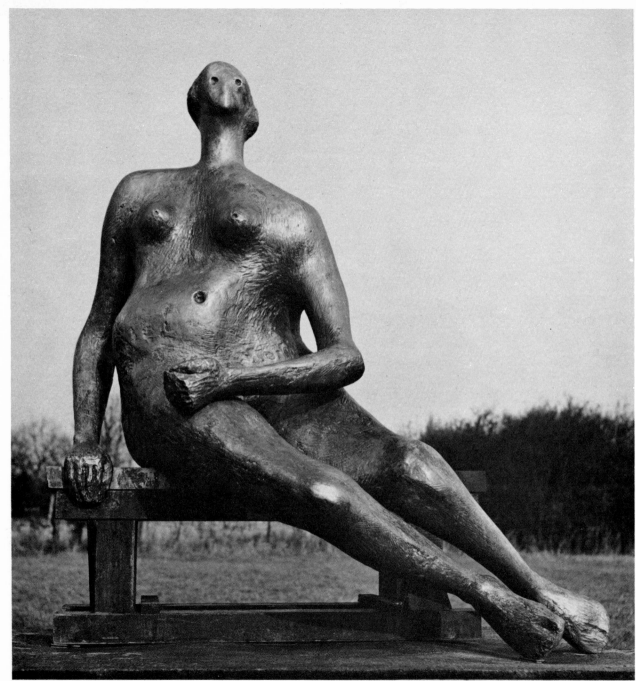

119 Seated woman 1957, height 57 in.

120 Falling warrior 1956–7, length 58 in.

121 Woman 1957–8, height 60 in. (detail)

122 Falling warrior 1956–7, length 58 in. (d

123 Working model for Locking piece 1962, height 42 in.

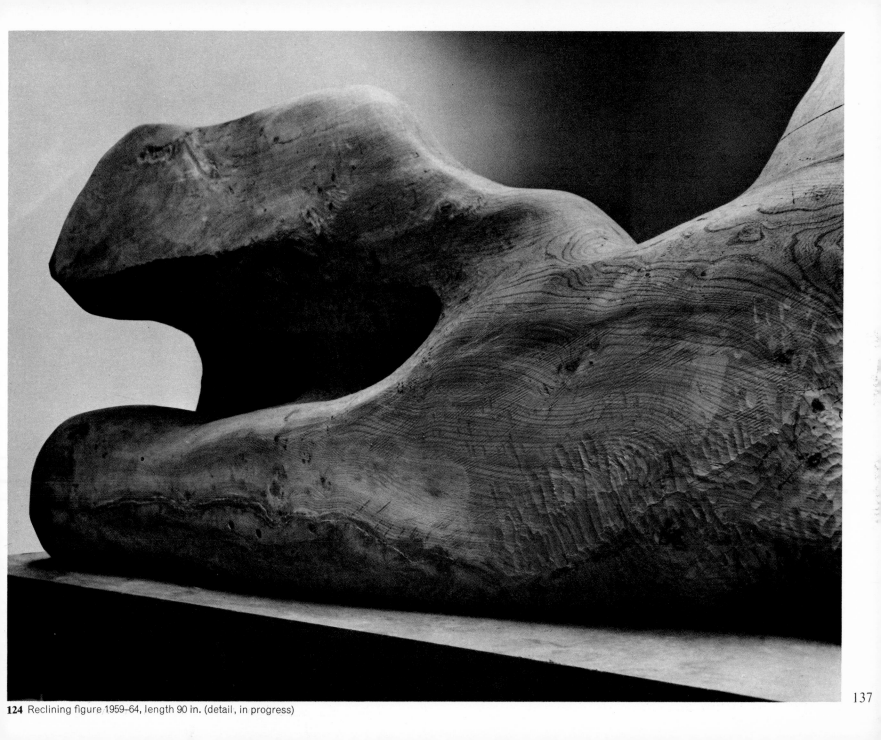

124 Reclining figure 1959–64, length 90 in. (detail, in progress)

125 Reclining figure 1959–64, length 90 in.

126 Reclining figure 1959–64, length 90 in.

Fitting Together

In recent years Moore has made several sculptures in which separate pieces are fitted together, married, in some way or another. It's a development with certain approximate precedents in Arp (167). In some works the pieces are detachable units, in others they are welded into one. The latter are anticipated in Moore's first more or less abstract sculpture (31): the figure's torso consists of two forms of which the upper is as it were suspended within and clasped by the lower. When creating the *Upright Motives* of 1955–6 (130), Moore started the sketch-models by balancing different forms one above the other as if building totem poles. In the finished products some of the forms are simply mounted upon one another; others fit into one another. It seems unlikely that structures of this kind could ever have come about so long as Moore was using drawing as his 'means of generating ideas for sculpture'.[1] But drawing had lately come to be superseded as his habitual way of beginning by the practice of playing about with forms in the round – especially found stones and bones. It was through toying with two stones and finding that they happened to interlock that Moore got the idea for the *Locking Piece* of 1962 (129), while the hand-size *Slow Form: Tortoise* of the same year (128) was realized by interlocking five units modelled on part of a stone and made as

alike as was compatible with their fitting together.

The changing interrelationships of the parts of the *Locking Piece* as one moves around it quite remarkably sustain their capacity to surprise. This is one of the few images Moore has realized in both medium-size and large versions which works about equally well as both. The version 42 inches high (123, 129) relates itself to human scale as something to be manipulated: one feels one's arm muscles straining as if one were twisting it round to unlock the pieces. The version nearly 10 feet high (127, 131, 134) gives an impression of impregnable density and overwhelming weight, also provokes the sort of wonder engendered by the walls of a fortress that it seems both a part of nature and man-made.

In some of the sculptures where parts that fit together remain separable, the conjunction occurs at only one or two points, as in certain two-piece sculptures in which one piece simply rests upon the other (133, 141) or a three-piece reclining figure in which one part clasps another at two points (132). But there are others in which the parts are wrapped around each other almost as fully as in the *Locking Piece* – two- and three-piece compositions (135, 137, 140) with forms suggesting a coupling and an intermingling of limbs. Finally, there are sculptures where one part

fits into a hole in another. The development is already hinted at in one of Moore's earliest two-piece carvings (136). This composition of 1934 also foreshadows, as we have observed, the internal/external sculptures, by suggesting the possibility that the hollowed piece might be extended to enclose the compact piece. But it also suggests the possibility that the compact piece could be jammed into the hollow (and the suggestion comes quite independently of recognition that the internal shape of the open piece is one of the most precisely sexual images in Moore's work). In the *Reclining Mother and Child* of 1960–1, the back of the internal form emerges through one of the openings in the back of the external form (25). In the *Three Rings* of 1966–7 (138, 139), the outside rings fit into the middle ring. Penetration and enclosure are implied: the concept of forms fitting together overlaps with that of internal and external forms. There is a feeling of movement of one within another, only it is uncertain whether this is of entrance or emergence.

127 Locking piece 1963–4, height 115½ in. (detail)

14

128 Slow form: Tortoise 1962, length 8½ in.

129 Working model for Locking piece 1962, height 42 in.

130 Upright motives Nos.1, 2 and 7 1955–6, height 132 in., 126 in., 126 in. (detail)

131 Locking piece 1963–4, height 115½ in.

132 Three-piece reclining figure No.2: Bridge prop 1963, length 99 in.

133 Two-piece sculpture: Pipe 1966, length 37 in.

134 Locking piece 1963–4, height 115½ in. (detail)

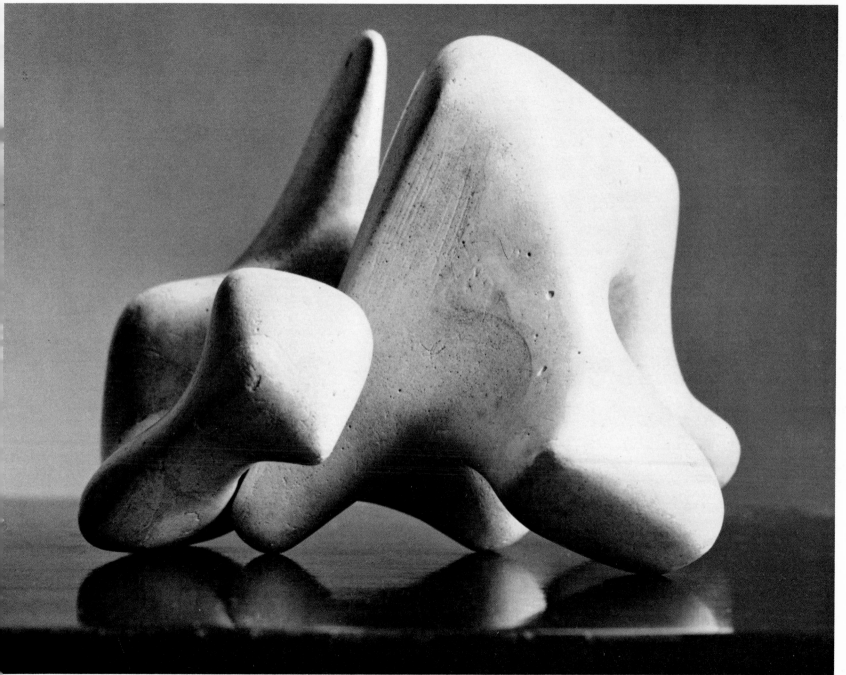

135 Sketch-model for Two-piece sculpture No. 11: Variation on one form 1968, length 4 in.

136 Two forms 1934, length 21 in.

137 Sketch-model for Two-piece sculpture No. 11: Variation on one form 1968, length 4 in.

138 Three rings 1966—7, length 106 in.

139 Three rings 1966, length 39 in.

140 Sketch-model for Three-piece sculpture: Vertebrae 1968, length 7½ in.

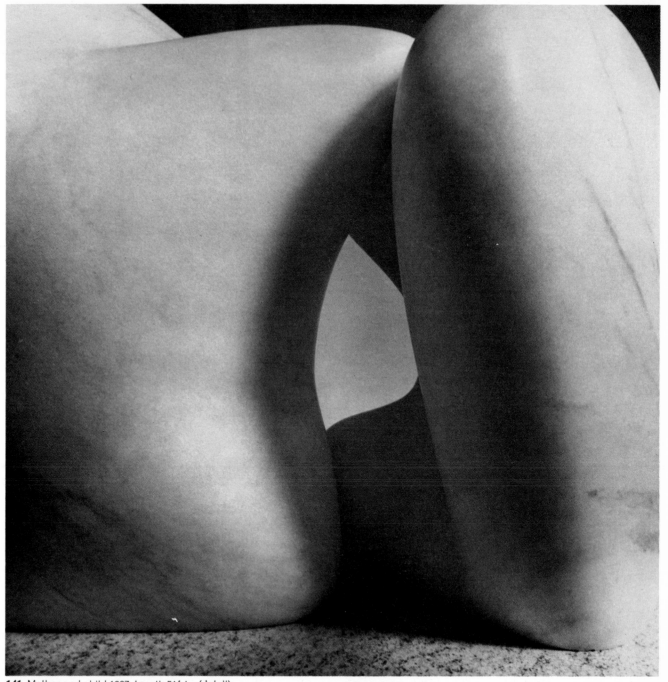

141 Mother and child 1967, length 51¼ in. (detail)

Notes

The Reclining Figure

1 *Architectural Association Journal*, vol. XLV, no. 519. London, May 1930. p. 408. The mountains idea came from Gaudier-Brzeska: "Sculptural energy is the mountain". (*Blast* no. 1. London, 1914. p. 155).

2 *The Listener*, vol. XVIII, no. 449. London, 18 August 1937. p. 339.

3 Quoted by J. D. Morse, *Magazine of Art*, vol. 40, no. 3. Washington D,C., March 1947. p. 101.

4 *Unit 1*, ed. Herbert Read. London (Cassell), 1934. p. 29.

5 One figure which has a pose quite impossible to achieve, as against the many with postures difficult to hold, is the Tate's Hornton stone piece of 1938 (8): of all the reclining figures, it is probably the one which seems the most majestically relaxed. (The elm recliner of 1959–64 (9), which appears to have a transitional, even uneasy, pose, is one of the figures whose pose can be most comfortably sustained.)

6 *The Listener*, vol. XIII, no. 334. London, 5 June 1935. p. 944.

7 *The Listener*, vol. XXV, no. 641. London, 24 April 1941. p. 598.

8 *Ibid*. p. 598.

9 *The Listener*, 5 June, 1935. p. 944.

10 *Unit 1*, 1934. p. 29.

11 In an interview by William Fagg, *Man*, vol. LI, no. 165. London (Royal Anthropological Institute), 1951. p. 96.

12 Walter Lehmann, *Altmexicanische Kunstgeschichte*, Berlin (Verlag Ernst Wasmuth A.G.), 1922. pl. 45. The reproduction here (144) is of this photograph.

Moore remembers seeing the illustration in Zwemmer's bookshop, probably around 1927. He looked at the plaster cast of the same statue in the Musée du Trocadéro in Paris only after completing the 1929 carving. He believes that he may have done so before making the 1930 carving. If this was the case, it could explain why the later piece is the one which more nearly resembles the prototype in its pose while being stylistically the more removed. It is the more removed largely because it owes more to nature. Thus the head of the 1929 figure is an ideal head, derived from the museums; the head of the 1930 figure is almost as much a portrait of the artist's wife – they were married in 1929 – as is, say, the large life-drawing in oils of 1929 of a half-length seated nude in the Whitworth Art Gallery, Manchester. On the other hand, according to Bernard Meadows, this head also resembles a Romanesque head on a córbel in the clerestory of Norwich Cathedral which Moore could well have seen during his summers in Norfolk.

13 Quoted by J. J. Sweeney, *Partisan Review*, vol. XIV, no. 2. New York, March–April 1947. pp. 180, 182.

14 For one thing, this is the first of Moore's many reclining figures to exhibit a mannerism constantly found in Michelangelo: a thigh is elongated and articulated in such a way as to provide the figure with an extra angle half-way between hip and knee.

15 In the metal statuette (71), it is the far knee that is the more bent, as with the river-gods. In the Hornton stone carving (8), the near knee is the one that is more bent – it's this above all that makes the pose anatomically impossible.

16 *The Listener*, 24 April 1941. p. 599.

The Mother and Child

1 The Hornton stone *Mother and Child* (17), begun in the autumn of 1924, was in fact not quite completed when he left for Italy at the end of January 1925, and was finished shortly after his return.

2 In a letter of 1943 an extract from which was first published in a leaflet issued by St. Matthew's Church. Reprints include *Henry Moore on Sculpture*, ed. Philip James, London (Macdonald), 1966. p. 220.

3 *The Listener*, 24 April 1941. p. 598.

4 *The Listener*, 18 August 1937. p. 339.

Correspondences

1 *Ibid*. p. 338

2 *Cahiers d'Art*, 3rd year, no. 7. Paris, 1928. p. 289. Photographs of two views are reproduced.

3 Several were reproduced in a Picasso number of *Documents*, vol. II, no. 3, Paris, 1930, of which there is a copy in Moore's library.

4 Reproduced in *Minotaure*, no. 1. Paris, 1933. pp. 33–7.

5 In fact the points are not separated in some of the casts (there are unique casts in lead and in iron, and an edition of bronzes).

6 This toy, which Moore knew as a child, consists of two interlocking pieces of cast metal between which is placed a cap that goes off when the bomb is dropped.

7 *Architectural Association Journal*, May 1930. p. 408.

8 This work was given the title *Mountains* when illustrated in R. H. Wilenski, *The Meaning of Modern Sculpture*. London (Faber), 1932. pl. 24.

9 *The Listener*, 8 August 1937. p. 339.

10 V. Donald Hall, *Henry Moore*. New York (Harper and Row), 1965. pp. 158–160. Adel Crag is illustrated.

Stones, Bones, Shells

1 *Unit 1*, 1934. p. 29.

2 This and the quotes at the start of the next four paragraphs are successive sentences from *Ibid.* pp 29–30.

3 *Architectural Association Journal*, May 1930. p. 408.

4 *The Listener*, 18 August 1937. p. 340.

5 He would have had a motive for doing so inasmuch as the 1934 text was written for the volume celebrating the formation of Unit 1, of which Nicholson was a fellow-member.

6 *The Listener*, 18 August 1937. p. 338.

7 In an interview by D. Sylvester, *The Listener*, vol. LXX, no. 1706. London, 29 August 1963. p. 306.

8 *The Listener*, 18 August 1937. p. 339.

9 Moore had previously made compositions with old sketch-models – dating from the mid-30s – when building possible models in 1952 for another commissioned relief: the screen for the new Time-Life building in London.

Holes and Hollows

1 In point of fact he wrote "Pebbles and rocks . . ." in 1934. *Unit 1*. p. 29.

2 *The Listener*, 18 August 1937. p. 339.

3 *Ibid.*, p. 339.

4 This piece was inspired by a ceremonial clay object from Babylon of *c*.2000 B.C. in the British Museum (B.M. 92,668). It is in the shape of a liver and is inscribed with magical formulae. It is reproduced in Christian Zervos, *L'Art de la Mésopotamie*, Paris (Editions 'Cahiers d'Art'), 1935, (n.p.), a book which Moore reviewed (*The Listener*, 5 June 1935. pp. 944–6).

Divided Figures

1 Quoted by Carlton Lake, *Atlantic Monthly*, vol. 209, no. 1. Boston, January 1962. p. 44.

2 *The Listener*, 29 August 1963. p. 306.

3 *Ibid.*, p. 306. Here "backbone" has been substituted for "vertebra" in the original published text.

Strings

1 *The Listener*, 18 August 1937. p. 339.

Draped

1 From a recorded talk, ed. R. Melville, issued by the British Council in 1955. First printed in Philip James, *op. cit.* p. 103.

2 *E.g.*, the facsimile of an MS. statement in Will Grohmann, *Henry Moore*, Berlin (Rembrandt Verlag), 1960. p. 266. Moore here identifies the conflict between the rival attractions of Mexican art, etc. and of Italian art (Cf. p.7) with a conflict between the 'tough' and the 'tender' 'opposing sides' in himself.

3 The dichotomy in 1931–2 was between the last of his early figurative pieces and his first somewhat abstract pieces. In 1936 it was between the stone carvings, with their abstract, compact, squarish forms, and the two reclining figures in elm wood with their rounded and opened-out forms.

4 Catalogue of *Sculpture in the open air, 1954*. London (L.C.C.), 1954. Note on cat. no. 21.

Hard and Soft

1 *Architectural Association Journal*, May 1930. p. 408.

2 Quoted in Warren Forma, *Five British Sculptors (work and talk)*. New York (Grossman), 1964. p. 59. I have taken the liberty of modifying the punctuation.

3 *Unit 1*, 1934. p. 30.

4 This shows, for example, in the extreme emphasis he has come to place upon the *Rondanini Pietà* when talking about Michelangelo. (*V.e.g.*, 'The Michelangelo Vision', an interview by D. Sylvester, *The Sunday Times Magazine*, London, 16 February 1964. pp. 18–23.) A postcard to the writer in 1952 describes the *Palestrina Pietà* as 'what I think is about the best of M.A.'s works'. In recent years one has scarcely heard him mention it.

Fitting Together

1 *The Listener*, 18 August 1937. p. 339.

Photographic Credits

All the photographs of Henry Moore's sculpture are by the artist with the following exceptions:
Vladimir Fyman 111
Errol Jackson 12, 13, 22
C. J. Laughlin 30
Lidbrooke 19, 66, 105
Simon Reed 87, 88

Comparative material
Alinari/Mansell Collection 149, 154
Anderson/Mansell Collection 142, 145, 147, 148
Courtauld Institute 160
Patricia O'Connell 166
Etienne Bertrand Weil 163
No. 155 is reproduced from *Cahiers d'Art*, 1928, p. 289
No. 157 is reproduced from *Minotaure* No. 1, 1933, pp. 36–7
No. 165 is reproduced from *Cahiers d'Art*, 1929, p. 350
No. 168 Crown copyright. Science Museum, London
Artist's copyright in Nos. 157, 158 and 165 is held by S.P.A.D.E.M. Paris, 1968

Comparative Material

142 Roman, 1st century A.D. *River Tiber*.
Piazza del Campidoglio, Rome

143 Greek, 5th century B.C. *Dionysus*.
From the Parthenon. British Museum

144 Toltec-Maya, 11th–12th century A.D. *Chacmool*. From Chichén Itzá. Museo Nacional
de Antropología, Mexico

145 Michelangelo. *Dawn*. Medici Chapel, Florence

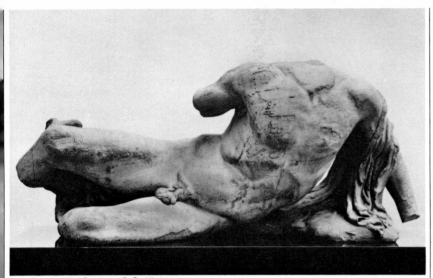

146 Greek, 5th Century B.C. *Ilissus*.
From the Parthenon. British Museum

147 Michelangelo. Detail from *The Conversion of Saint Paul*.
Pauline Chapel, Rome

148 Michelangelo. *Night*. Medici Chapel, Florence

149 Giotto. Detail from *The Ognissanti Madonna*.
Ufizzi, Florence

150 Masaccio. Detail from *The Virgin and Child*.
National Gallery, London

151 Raphael. Detail from *The Ansidei Madonna*.
National Gallery, London

152 Greek, 6th Century B.C. Seated figure from the Sacred Way at Miletus. British Museum

153 Moore. The Northampton Madonna and Child in progress

154 Michelangelo. *The Rondanini Pietà*. Castello Sforzesco, Milan

155 Picasso. *Metamorphosis*, 1928.
The artist

156 Brancusi. *The Princess*, 1916.
Philadelphia Museum of Art. Arensberg Coll.

157 Picasso. Two pages from *An Anatomy*, 1933. The artist

158 Picasso. *Horse's head*, 1937. On extended loan to the
Museum of Modern Art, New York

159 School of Fontainebleau, 16th century. Detail from *Gabrielle d'Estrées and
her sister in the bath*. Louvre, Paris

160 Picasso. *Glass of absinthe*, 1914.
Private collection, Paris

161 Brancusi. *Chimera*, 1918. Philadelphia Museum of Art.
Louise and Walter Arensberg Collection

162 Archipenko. *Walking woman*, 1912.
Denver Art Museum

163 Arp. *Bell and navels*, 1931

164 Giacometti. *Project for a piazza*, c.1930–1.
Peggy Guggenheim Collection, Venice

165 Picasso. Drawing: project for a monument, 1928

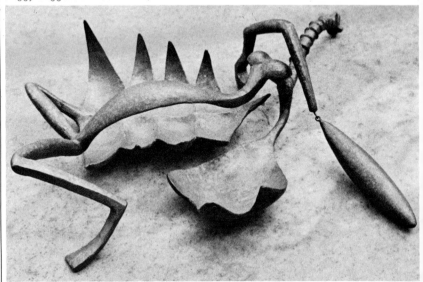

166 Giacometti. *Slaughtered woman*, 1932

167 Arp. Hybrid fruit called Pagoda, 1934.
Tate Gallery.

168 Stringed surface model: hyperbolic paraboloid.
Science Museum, London

165

Index of Illustrations

Sculpture and drawings are listed separately, each in chronological order
The number (or numbers) in bold at the end of each entry refers to the illustration(s)
No collection details are given for bronzes (other than unique casts)

Sculpture

W - W.
10-76